P9-CEM-158

PROPERTY OF
ARKANSAS LIBRARY COMMISSION
506½ Center Street
LITTLE ROCK, ARKANSAS

Twayne's United States Authors Series

Harold Frederic

HAROLD FREDERIC

by THOMAS F. O'DONNELL
Utica College of Syracuse University

and

HOYT C. FRANCHERE
Portland State College

Twayne Publishers, Inc. :: New York

Library of Congress Catalog Card Number: 61-9857

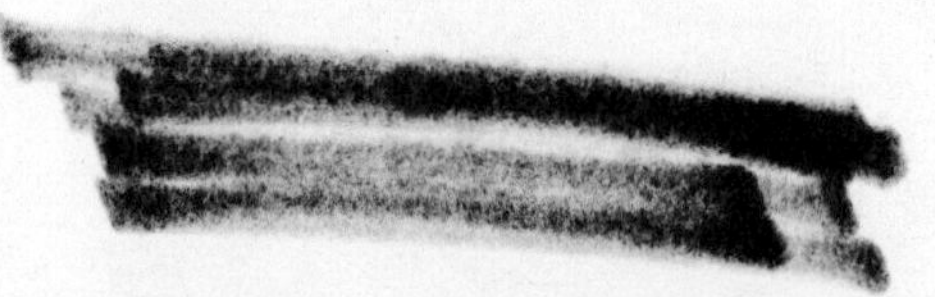

MANUFACTURED IN THE UNITED STATES OF AMERICA BY
UNITED PRINTING SERVICES, INC.
NEW HAVEN, CONN.

To

Gert and Ruth

Preface

THE INTENT of *Harold Frederic* is to place before the general reader and the student of American literature a study of a journalist and author who, after his death in England in 1898, was consigned to an ignominious obscurity from which he has only recently been released. Though we have no wish to raise Frederic to a rank out of proportion to his merit, we do believe that his work has stature and significance and that he deserves a fairer judgment as a writer than has so far been given him. We believe, too, that the modern reader who turns to the whole canon of his creative fiction will find in it much that compares favorably with the best writing of his era. The range of Frederic's novels and short stories encompasses the romantic as well as the realistic, the tragic as well as the comic, the ancient as well as the contemporary.

With only one or two exceptions, the general surveys of American literature have almost ignored Harold Frederic; they have dismissed him as a writer of potboilers; or they have uncritically followed the evaluations of writers whose reading of Frederic has been limited. One critic of American literature was in fact so careless in the examination of a Frederic novelette as to make a "village coquette" out of the hero of the story, an astounding metamorphosis. Error has thus been compounded by error. In this volume we have therefore tried (1) to portray Harold Frederic, the man, as a three-dimensional figure, both in his New York and in his London environments; (2) to revise some critical estimates and to render unhurried judgments of his best-known fictions; and (3) to give him his rightful place among American writers of the latter nineteenth century.

We are happy to record the names of those who generously gave us their assistance and encouragement as we prepared this volume: Miss Lillian Gilkes, who shared not only her deep interest in our project but also her scholarly researches in the Crane-Frederic relationship; Mrs. Eliot Keen, Mr. Harold Frederic, Mr. Clifton Waller Barrett, Mr. Barry Forman, Mr. Ames W. Williams, and Mrs. A. Spencer Hughes, who supplied us with Frederic letters as well as with notes, pictures, and memoranda so important to this study; Sir Alfred Watson, Vice-President of the National Liberal Club, London, whose reminiscences about Frederic's club life were invaluable; Mr. Coss Billson, Secretary to the National Liberal Club; Mr. and Mrs. Harold Mortlake (in their unforgettable bookshop at 24 Cecil Court, off Charing Cross Road).

Grateful acknowledgment is made also for grants given one of the authors of *Harold Frederic*: from the American Philosophical Society, a grant that made possible both travel and research in London; and from Portland State College, a grant that permitted the acquisition of certain valuable documents.

We wish to thank the librarians and curators of special collections at the Butler Library, Columbia University; the New York Public Library; the New York State Library at Albany; the Library of Congress; the Library of Harvard University; the British Museum and the Colindale branch of the British Museum; the Pennsylvania Historical Society; and the Library of the University of Southern California.

Some special thanks are due our friends and colleagues, especially Professors Arthur W. Brown and Charles E. Samuels of Utica College, for ideas and encouragement over the years. We shall ever be grateful to Professor Edwin Cady of Indiana University, who, knowing of our mutual interest in Harold Frederic, brought us together.

T.F. O'D.
H.C.F.

Utica, New York
Portland, Oregon
November, 1960

Contents

Chapter

	Chronology	11
1.	"Dearborn County" Boyhood, 1856-1871	17
2.	The Young Journalist, 1871-1884	31
3.	Foreign Correspondent and Author, 1884-1898	50
4.	Before the Damnation	73
5.	*The Damnation of Theron Ware*	108
6.	Aristocrats and Buccaneers	118
7.	Summation: Marks of Greatness	141
	Notes and References	164
	Selected Bibliography	176
	Index	180

Chronology

1856 Harold Frederic born August 19, only son of Henry DeMott and Frances Ramsdell Frederick, in Utica, New York.

1858 Frederic's father, a freight conductor on the New York Central, was killed in a train accident.

1860 Frederic's mother married her husband's cousin, William DeMott.

1871 Frederic graduated from the Advanced School in Utica on July 6. Began work as a printer and negative retoucher for local photographers.

1873 Went to Boston where, continuing his trade in photography, he also studied art as an avocational interest.

1875 Returned to Utica to become proofreader for the Utica *Morning Herald.*
In December, joined the staff of the Utica *Observer*, the leading Democratic daily west of Albany.

1877 On June 30, published his first story in the *Observer*: "The Blakelys of Poplar Place. A Legend of the Mohawk."
On October 10, married Grace Williams, daughter of David and Ruth Green Williams and granddaughter of Beriah Green, famous abolitionist. Grace's mother, ill at the time, died two days later.

1878 A daughter, Ruth, born to Grace and Harold.

1880 Became editor of the Utica *Observer.*

1882 Appointed editor of the Albany *Evening Journal*, a traditionally Republican paper founded by Thurlow Weed. After three weeks, Frederic effected a "bolting" from the Republicanism of his daily, an action that helped to elect Grover Cleveland as Governor of New York. Became close friend of Cleveland.

Frederic assumed his duties on September 4. His family joined him several months later.

1884 The *Journal*, sold in March, was returned politically to its strictly Republican position and Frederic was out of a job.

Applied for work with the New York *Times* and was given the post of London correspondent. In June, sailed with his family for England.

On July 27, his dispatch for the *Times*, "Down Among the Dead Men," written after his five-day tour of the cholera-ridden cities of Toulon, Marseilles, and Arles, made him something of a hero among his newspaper colleagues and gave him an international reputation.

Joined the Savage Club, sponsored by Aaron Watson and supported by the personal recommendation of Grover Cleveland.

1884-1898 Published articles and stories in English and American magazines, including *The Fortnightly Review, The Idler, The English Illustrated Magazine, The Bookman, Pall Mall Gazette, Pall Mall Budget, The Saturday Review, Cosmopolitan, Harper's New Monthly Magazine, The Youth's Companion, Scribner's Magazine, The Saturday Evening Post,* and others.

1885 Elected to the National Liberal Club in which he did not become active until 1886. There met such men as Gladstone, David Lloyd George, Parnell, and many other British and Irish statesmen and members of Parliament and became the intimate of many of these men.

A son, Harold, born to the Frederics on July 10.

1886 Sold *Seth's Brother's Wife* to Scribner's.

Moved his family to Bedford Square, a short distance from the British Museum.

1887 *Seth's Brother's Wife* serialized in *Scribner's Magazine;* published by Scribner's in April and by Chatto and Windus in London on November 17.

A second son, Hereward, born on January 27.

1889 The first Harold died. Another son, born September 15, was named Harold.
Became active in the Ghouls Club whose membership included such distinguished men as James M. Barrie, W. E. Henley, Joseph Pennell, and other writers and artists. They met in High Holborn, only a short walk from Frederic's Bedford Square residence.

1890 *In the Valley,* serialized in *Scribner's Magazine,* published in New York by Scribner's, in London by Heinemann.
The Lawton Girl published in New York by Scribner's, in London by Chatto and Windus.
Met and fell in love with Kate Lyon, apparently while working in the British Museum. Established a second household, called "Homefield," in Kenley, a part of the Coulsdon parish in Surrey, about fifteen miles south of London, continuing this relationship through the rest of his life.

1891 Published *The Young Emperor, William II of Germany*: G. P. Putnam's Sons in New York and T. F. Unwin in London.

1892 *The New Exodus,* a collection of Frederic's *Times* dispatches, published by Putnam's in New York, by Heinemann in London. The work concerns a Jewish pogrom in Russia. Frederic's reporting so effective that Czar banned him from further travel in that country.
The Return of the O'Mahony published by R. Bonner's Sons in New York, by Heinemann in London.
The first of three children, Helen, born to Kate Lyon; the others were Héloise, 1893, and Barry, 1894.
Moved Grace and her children to Claremont Gardens, Surbiton, in southwest London.

1893 *The Copperhead,* serialized in *Scribner's Magazine,* published by Scribner's in New York. With other stories, it was published by Heinemann in London.

1894 *Marsena and Other Stories* published by Scribner's in New York. "The Deserter" appeared in serial form in *The Youth's Companion.*

1895 Probably moved Grace and her children to Old House, Brook Green, in the Hammersmith District, London; the first listing of this address does not appear in *Kelly's Directories* until 1897.

1896 *The Damnation of Theron Ware,* considered Frederic's greatest novel, published by Stone and Kimball in Chicago. Under its English title, *Illumination,* published by Heinemann in London.
March Hares published first in this year under Frederic's pseudonym, George Forth, by John Lane in London and by D. Appleton and Company in New York.

1898 *Gloria Mundi,* serialized in the *Cosmopolitan,* published by Stone in Chicago, by Heinemann in London. In August, Frederic suffered a stroke. He died on October 19.

1899 *The Market-Place,* serialized in the *Saturday Evening Post,* published posthumously by Frederick A. Stokes in New York, by Heinemann in London.

Harold Frederic

CHAPTER 1

"Dearborn County" Boyhood, 1856-1871

THE CITY of Utica—the "Octavius" of Harold Frederic's fiction—lies near the western end of New York's picturesque Mohawk Valley, settling on the south bank of the river that here moves placidly toward the Hudson, ninety miles to the east. Across the river, always in view of the city, swell the Deerfield hills, small brothers of the Adirondacks farther on and out of sight. Along the base of these hills, first on the river itself and rude roads, then on the Erie Canal that cut through what was the heart of the city, and finally on the railroads and major turnpikes that stretched across the width of the state, a fifth of a nation made its way westward in the decades after the Revolution as it followed the only water-level route through the northern Appalachians.

In Utica, in a large frame house on the edge of a city of 20,000 and about two miles from the river that gives the valley its name, Harold Frederic was born on August 19, 1856.[1] In this city and for most of the time in this house, Frederic lived his first twenty-eight years—two-thirds of his entire life. During the final third until his death in London in 1898, the house, the city, and the valley were never far from his mind or heart. All three—and an occasional picture of Frederic himself as a boy or young man—appear in various guises in his American fiction from *Seth's Brother's Wife* to *The Damnation of Theron Ware*.

Frederic's mature memories of this native city and countryside—"Dearborn County," as he called the area in his novels and stories—were always to be vivid and pleasant. For in Utica in 1875, as an ambitious nineteen-year-old proofreader, he began a newspaper career that was to bring him international recognition within ten years. And, even more important, in Utica he began a training that was ultimately to shape him into upstate New York's most significant literary artist since James Fenimore Cooper.

I

Few American writers have been more deeply rooted in their native soil than Harold Frederic. His father, Henry DeMott Frederick (Frederic was later to drop the *k* from his name), could greet his newborn son as the most recent of a line that began in America with an early Dutch colonial progenitor, Henrich Fredericksz, a sturdy farm laborer who in 1633 settled on one of the patroon's farms near what is now Albany.[2] By 1856, the Fredericks had been living in upstate New York—always along either the Hudson or the Mohawk and within a day's journey from Albany—for eight generations. They were a quiet, industrious breed of men: farmers through the early generations; later tradesmen and artisans, coopers, cobblers, and cabinetmakers.

Also through his father, Harold Frederic was descended from the DeMotts, a Palatine German family whose name is spelled variously in colonial documents as Teymouth, Damoth, and Dimuth. The DeMott line had begun in America in 1710, when a group of refugees from the Rhineland Palatinate arrived in New York City. By 1722 a number of them, including John Jost Teymouth, had settled on the rich lowlands along the Mohawk River in what is now Herkimer County.[3]

If Harold Frederic inherited from his Dutch ancestors a love for the land and a feeling for craftsmanship, from his Palatine forebears he inherited other, different traits: a strong sense of adventure, a sturdy independence, and even a taste for battle. For the DeMotts, unlike the Fredericks, were warriors as well as pioneers. Old John Jost Teymouth and his sons, carving their farm from wilderness near what is now Little Falls, had harassed and been harassed by angry Mohawks. Another generation had drummed stolidly off to little wars against the French and Indians, who periodically swooped into the valley and scarred the peace and prosperity of what was then Sir William Johnson's domain. Two of Frederic's

DeMott forebears were actually taken prisoner on such raids, one by the French and the other by Indians, although both later returned safely from captivity. A third, Captain Mark Damuth, was part of the motley band of Mohawk Valley farmers who followed their neighbor, Nicholas Herkimer, into "Bloody Gulch" at Oriskany on an August day in 1777. Captain Mark, unlike General Herkimer himself, lived to talk about the fierce day's fighting.[4]

Some time in or about 1819, these two family lines merged when Matilda DeMott married a young cooper named Henry Frederick, whose Dutch family had lived more quietly than the DeMotts, and farther east in the valley. This marriage produced a number of sons, including Henry DeMott Frederick, the father of Harold Frederic.

Through his mother, Frederic came from another family that had been scarcely less active than his father's in shaping the character of the Mohawk Valley. "All four of my great-grandfathers bore arms in the Revolutionary War," Frederic was to write in 1897, "and one of them indeed somewhat indefinitely expanded this record by fighting on both sides. My earliest recollections are of tales told by my grandmother about local heroes of this conflict who were but middle-aged people when she was a child."[5] Which of his four embattled ancestors fought "on both sides" can only be guessed, but there is no doubt about the grandmother. She was Lucretia Newland Ramsdell, who was fifty-seven years old at the birth of her grandson, widowed, and as self-reliant as any woman in the valley. Later, when she moved into the Frederic home on South Street during the Civil War years, Grandmother Ramsdell related many exciting tales of Revolutionary days to her eager grandson, young Harry Frederic. She could tell him of her own father, John Newland, another soldier in the Revolution; or she could tell him about her husband's father, Moses Ramsdale, who had served as a drummer boy in the Fourth Regiment of the New York line before settling on land near what was later to be Utica.[6] As he grew to manhood, Harry Frederic was to hear more about old Moses Ramsdale, whose legendary strength had won for him the reputation as the strongest man in the Mohawk Valley. And in *The Damnation of Theron Ware* he was to memorialize the name of Ramsdell by inverting it, dropping a letter, and bestowing it upon one of his most memorable characters—the suave and erudite scientist, Dr. Ledsmar.

These, then, were Harold Frederic's people, a group of sturdy ancestors among whom there were few to worship but many to admire: eight generations of middle-class farmers, craftsmen, and pioneer-soldiers who had played minor roles in the drama of New York colonial and state history. All together, they had little but a supply of their own middle-class virtues to pass on to this newest member of the clan—no family tradition of learning, such as Emerson, for example, had inherited; no sense of family guilt, like Hawthorne's; no overpowering religious heritage to brood over and rebel against in the manner of Stephen Crane. There were no artists, no preachers, no scholars in Harold Frederic's ancestry—only common men who, on occasion, gave up their plows or tools reluctantly to go to war, and women who waited for their return. As flesh and blood forebears most of them are now faceless; and only a thin family tradition or two remained, even in Frederic's youth, to hint that, like the forgotten Fairchilds of *Seth's Brother's Wife* at rest in in the forlorn family cemetery, "they had been alive, and now were dead."

But as abstractions and as shadowy figures whose movements added depth to the dramatic development of his own society, these ancestors were to be important to Harold Frederic. The reader meets them again and again in the explicitly historical fiction from "The Blakelys of Poplar Place" through the Civil War stories, but most obviously in *In the Valley.* There, in the character of Douw Mauverensen, Frederic drew a picture of himself as he might have been had be been born a century earlier, rather than on August 19, 1856.

II

Henry DeMott Frederick had every right to be proud of the fine house in which his new son was born. Among the few frame houses that had recently been raised on South Street, the Fredericks' was not only one of the newest but one of the biggest. In its three ample Victorian stories there would be plenty of room for the family that the Fredericks presumably expected to have. The young couple had not always lived in such roomy quarters. For a time after their marriage, which occurred probably in 1850, they had lived with Grandmother Ramsdell in her house at 44 Elizabeth Street. Then one day Henry Frederick had boldly given up his job as a chair-finisher to go to California with his new wife's brother-in-law, John Baxter, to prospect for gold. This junket, destined to be the one big adventure in Henry Frederick's life, met with moderate success; and the young husband returned to Utica with enough money to move his bride into their house on South Street some time in 1853. Now, his curiosity apparently satisfied about the world outside the Mohawk Valley, Henry Frederick went back to his chair-finishing; and Frances Ramsdell Frederick went about keeping the big house in order.[7]

Two years later, however, Henry Frederick was unhappy or ill, or both. In 1855, after complaining about the confining nature of his work and blaming his failing health on the shellac fumes that were his daily atmosphere, he once more abandoned chair-finishing. This time, unable or unwilling to go west himself, he did the next best thing: he took a job as freight-conductor on the New York Central. In 1855, a good percentage of the "freight" was human—immigrants bound for the West that Henry Frederick had once seen, but would never see again.

Harold Frederic was barely eighteen months old on a bitter February 23, 1858, when an unknown courier brought news to the house on South Street. Henry DeMott Frederick was dead—crushed beneath a careening empty freight car that had been derailed and hurled from the New York Central tracks near Amsterdam, sixty miles from Utica.[8] So died the young father that Harold Frederic never knew and was seldom to mention except by indirection: the boys in his fiction are almost invariably fatherless. And if he left little else to his infant son, Henry Demott Frederick had endowed the boy with a strain of restlessness that was to be part of his mature personality.

From pictures taken later, when this first tragedy of her life was only a sharp memory, Frances Ramsdell Frederick appears to have been a woman who could be touched but not shattered by grief. Still in her early twenties when she buried her first husband, Mrs. Frederick mourned him briefly and then went about the tasks of rearing her son and keeping the big house—about the only things that Henry had left behind. In both tasks, Frances had the hearty support of her own widowed mother, Lucretia Ramsdell, who still lived in solitary self-sufficiency on nearby Elizabeth Street.

Grandmother Ramsdell could teach her newly widowed daughter much about making her own way. For years she had supported her children by operating restaurants and boarding houses. By the time of her new grandson's birth, she had given up these and turned for a livelihood to the sewing machine—a device in which she shrewdly recognized a promising potential. If Frances Frederick had not been a skilled seamstress before her husband's death, she became one soon after under the tutelage of her vigorous mother. Before the memory of Henry Frederick had grown dim in the house, Frances was so busily making vests that she needed several young women to assist her. Because of her industry and acumen, there was no destitution in her son's early years.

Harold Frederic grew into boyhood in a world of many sounds: in the house, the steady whirring of sewing machines and his mother's harsh voice determined to be heard above all;[9] outside, the faraway shouts of canallers on the Erie or in the nearby basin, the whine of sawmills on the fringe of the city, the clatter of westbound carriage traffic on Genesee Street—the venerable Seneca Turnpike that stretched from Albany to Buffalo.

But much of the sound that he heard in the noisy city was talk, and it was always of war: when it would come, how it was going, how it had been. As a youngster of six or seven, he could have been a small part of the tense crowds that gathered periodically in the streets before Mechanics Hall to listen carefully as a clerk shouted newly drawn draft numbers from an open window on the second floor.[10] And he certainly must have been among enthusiastic well-wishers who lined the streets or gathered at the railroad station to wave farewell to Utica's departing contingents, one of which included his cousin, Joseph Baxter, going off to glory as a lieutenant of cavalry.[11] Scenes like these lingered in his mind and came alive again in "The Eve of the Fourth," "Marsena," and other tales of the Civil War.

During these war years before his ninth birthday in 1865, Frederic could also have noticed that not all the farmers who drove their rigs through the streets of Utica seemed to be so enthusiastic about the Union cause as the crowds gathered at the railway stations. He could have heard talk about "Copperheads"—southern sympathizers—in the hinterlands of Oneida County. In 1863 and 1864, he could have heard Governor Horatio Seymour, whose name was already revered in the Frederic home, damned as a Copperhead. Or, if he had been in the right place at the right time, he could have heard President Lincoln and the Union cause criticized by another group—diehard Abolitionists like old Beriah Green of Whitesboro, for instance—who still muttered angrily because the government tarried so long in striking for the slaves. Extremists of both stripes, less noisy of course than they had been in the forties and fifties, still walked the streets of Utica; and an alert boy like Harry Frederic could have sensed that not all the people around him were ardent Unionists.

Most of them were, however, and so there was no lack of huge bonfires for a boy to watch when news came over the wire of a significant or trivial Union victory. And when the news told of the honorable exploits of the 14th New York, an infantry regiment better known as the 1st Oneida, the city's joy was unconfined—unbounded, that is, until the casualty lists began to trickle in, bringing a sorrow that spread through the streets until even a boy could detect it.

War was an important part of Frederic's early youth, but not all of it; it was, rather, a kind of backdrop against which other important events occurred. Some time in 1861, for example, Frances Frederick left the South Street home for a brief and, to her son, mysterious trip to Oswego. When she returned, she brought with her a new husband, William H. DeMott, a pleasant-faced, mild-mannered distant cousin of Henry DeMott Frederick. Two or three years younger than his new wife, DeMott was a machinist by trade; he was to fit easily and quickly into the family and to play a real, if somewhat subdued, part in its continuing modest prosperity.[12] Exactly how young Harry Frederic responded to the realization that he now had a stepfather cannot be known. Certainly he was not actively resentful of the newcomer—not for long, at any rate. He evidently accepted the new situation quickly. His mother continued to be the strong force in the family and life was not much different from what it had been with "the widow Frederick."

At about the same time her daughter was acquiring a second husband, Grandmother Ramsdell, in her healthy sixties now, also moved into what was from now on to be called the DeMott home. The return of his grandmother was more important to five-year-old Harry Frederic than the acquisition of a quiet, retiring stepfather. For Grandmother Ramsdell not only told wonderful stories about the Revolutionary War that she had heard during her own childhood but also liked to steal off to the Basin occasionally to drop a line for bullheads or suckers; and she did not mind if her grandson tagged along after her.[13] And, when she moved into her daughter's home, Grandmother Ramsdell brought books that Harry soon learned to finger and eventually to read. If most of them were semi-scholarly accounts of Biblical customs, or accounts of travels in the Holy Land, or were concerned with various aspects of Methodist history, young Frederic did not mind. Some of them had pictures, and one—a copy of *Josephus*—he read again and again.[14]

Besides her religious books Grandmother Ramsdell also brought a more formal attitude toward religion itself than had previously prevailed in the DeMott home. Frances Frederick DeMott, to be sure, was a religious woman in a sense: she sang in a Presbyterian choir. Her new husband, William DeMott, was at least nominally a Presbyterian. But Grandmother Ramsdell was more religious than either of them; and after her coming, the spirit of the DeMott house was more Methodist than Presbyterian. This, indeed, was as it should have been; for the Fredericks, as well as the Ramsdells, had been active Methodists for decades. One of Harry's uncles, in fact, had been among the founders of the new Corn Hill Methodist Church, and Harry's own father had been its beadle for a short time before his death. Young Frederic, his elders decided, would be brought up a Methodist, like most of his family before him.[15]

The Corn Hill Church, a short walk from the DeMott home on South Street, was only a few years older than Harry himself when he became a member in the early 1860's. Already, however, its congregation was split into two quarreling factions, one of which—a small but stubbornly righteous minority—looked with strong disapproval on what it condemned as the growing worldliness of the majority group. Whatever he may have thought about the standard, traditional services that he attended, the testy bickering among older Methodists of the congregation made a permanent impression on Frederic's young mind.

Years later, in "Cordelia and the Moon," a short story that anticipates in some ways *The Damnation of Theron Ware,* the youthful narrator voices Frederic's own memories of the Corn Hill congregation when he says that "there had been struggles about whether the pastor should consent to be supplied with milk Sunday morning," and "whether it was fitting that his wife should wear artificial flowers in her bonnet." "About these and kindred matters," he goes on, "our church had wrangled ever since I could remember." The wranglers and the wrangling stayed in Frederic's memory; for such dour characters as Loren Pierce and Erastus Winch, joyless trustees of Theron Ware's church in Octavius, are fictional counterparts of members of the small group which finally seceded from the Corn Hill Church in 1863 and established its own Free Methodist Church in Utica.[16]

III

Against the backdrop of the Civil War, which was usually far away but at times ominously close to Utica, life went on in the DeMott household. Adults were free to spend much of their time arguing about the wisdom of Mr. Lincoln's choice of generals, about Horatio Seymour's chances in the next election, about whether or not John Wesley had said anything about organ music in his churches; but boys of Harry Frederic's age had to go to school.

In 1862, the year he probably started, Harry Frederic had even a shorter distance to walk than most of his fellows. Dressed in his Kossuth hat and Garibaldi jacket (clothes which reflected Frances DeMott's sympathies for rebels against foreign tyrannies), Harry merely had to go around the corner to Public School No. 12 on Seymour Avenue, practically within earshot of his mother's busy sewing machines. The principal of this small school was young Sarah Coventry, whose father (like Miss Stratford's in Frederic's Civil War story, "The Eve of the Fourth") was a well-known Utica physician. In this school and later in a new building nearer still to the DeMott home, Frederic remained until 1868. In the faces and the talk of his fellow pupils and perhaps of Miss Coventry, Frederic was to see, hear, and feel more dramatically than ever how the faraway war seared the lives of people who could only stand and wait.

Then, at last, the rumbling from the South that had been in his ears ever since he could remember was over, and all the talk turned to other things. But happy moments were devoted to greeting the Utica men who continued to trickle home after years of absence. Among the returning veterans were men who would change the character of the city in the aftermath of war. From 1865 on, Harold Frederic was to have remarkable opportunities to see, at first hand, how national issues and national leaders developed on the American scene.

Exactly when his interest in politics began to burgeon can hardly be determined. It may well have done so in 1866 during the spirited campaign that resulted in the election of General James McQuade as mayor of Utica. McQuade was a Democrat, a war hero, the colorful scion of a prosperous Irish family whose respectable fortune had been built on a successful whiskey known as "McQuade's Mountain Dew." Watching the parades of partisans, many of them uniformed veterans of McQuade's own proud 1st Oneida, listening to the adjective-laden speeches of McQuade supporters, thrilling to the sound of drums and the sight of torchlights on Genesee Street, Harry Frederic at the age of ten may well have concluded that a political campaign was a very exciting thing indeed. In any case, during the first few years after the war when Utica and America poised on the brink of the Gilded Age, he got his first impressive glimpses of an aspect of American life that was to attract his mature talents not only as a journalist but as a novelist.

In 1868 politics came to Utica on a grand scale when the Democratic National Convention nominated Horatio Seymour to oppose the overwhelming favorite, General Grant, for

President. Again there were parades, even noisier now, and stirring speeches, and an occasional glimpse of the elderly neighbor who *might* be going to the White House. Disappointed but not dejected when Seymour lost by a surprisingly small margin, Utica Democrats, including the DeMotts and youthful Harold Frederic, found consolation in the fact that "The Old Governor," as Frederic always called him, had carried New York State. Horatio Seymour remained even in defeat a hero on South Street.[17]

The election over, Uticans now returned to what they had been doing before the convention that almost gave them a President. By now, Frederic himself had other things than boys' games to occupy him. Some time in 1867, William and Frances DeMott had purchased a small wood and milk business; and Harry Frederic played a regular role in the family enterprise.[18] His mother now had less time than she could wish to devote to the business. A new baby, Helen DeMott, had joined the family, and the arrival of this half-sister added indirectly to Harry Frederic's responsibilities. Before and after school he worked with his stepfather or a hired man at the treadmill-saw; like Job Parshall in "The Deserter," he prepared the dairy cows for milking and learned to warm his chilled hands by burying them in a bin of oats; like Harvey Semple in *The Damnation of Theron Ware,* he delivered milk to dairy customers in the surrounding neighborhood and probably gossiped along the way. His morning chores done, he went to school. Until he was almost thirteen, walking to school took so little of his time that he could have stayed at chores practically until bell-time. For this reason, at least, he must have looked forward to the fall of 1869, when he finally entered the Advanced School and so got farther away from home and his mother's sharp eye.

Near the center of town, the Advanced School had a total enrollment of about 430 pupils, with girls in the majority. For some of Frederic's fellows, this school would be merely another step toward the Utica Academy where they would finish their public school education. But for most of them, including Frederic, the three years in the Advanced School would be the end: here they would receive the "good common school education" that ten women teachers and a male principal were prepared to give them. No haphazard nineteenth-century country schoolhouse, the Advanced School, like other units of the Utica system of public education, was staffed by teachers who were well qualified by prevailing standards and who followed a carefully planned syllabus.[19]

After school, on days when chores at home were light, a short walk on Genesee Street took Harry Frederic to the School District Library, which from 1856 until 1878, was housed in Utica's City Hall. Here he was free to browse among the approximately 5,800 volumes the library contained in 1870. Although he probably dipped into the liberally stocked shelves of both fiction and non-fiction in the library's juvenile section, the titles that he carried home and later remembered were substantial ones. The librarians must have been impressed by this schoolboy who charged out such formidable works as Horace Walpole's four-volume *Memoirs of the Reign of King George III* and Prosper Mérimée's two-volume *History of Peter the Cruel.*[20] Here also he could find histories of his own state and county: Mrs. Ann Grant's *Memoirs of an American Lady,* for instance, and Pomroy Jones' *Annals and Recollections of Oneida County,* both of them rich in anecdote and color. Benson G. Lossing's well-known works were there, too: *The Life and Times of Philip Schuyler*—a man who was later to be a kind of off-stage hero of *In the Valley*—the famous *Pictorial Field-Books* of the Revolution and the War of 1812, and later the *Pictorial History of the Civil War.*

In the Utica library he also could have become acquainted for the first time with translations of the fiction of the French collaborators, Emile Erckmann and Alexandre Chatrian, who were enjoying a wide vogue in the United States. "They dominated me at a time when it was of particular importance what influence I fell under," Frederic was to say of Erckmann-Chatrian's works in 1897. "They formed in my mind the symbol of writing."[21] Later, he assembled his own collection of Erckmann-Chatrian titles and was prompted to do so no doubt by the delight he had found in *Mme. Thérèse, The Conscript,* and *Waterloo*—all of which had been available to him in the Utica Library. And if he had cared to do so (there is no direct evidence that he did), he could have dipped into the library's liberal selection of contemporary fiction: new novels by William Dean Howells and Edward Eggleston, for instance, which stood side by side with standard editions of Scott, Dickens, Thackeray, Cooper, Irving, and Hawthorne.

Besides the fairly well-stocked library, there were other places in Utica where young Frederic augmented his education. As early as 1864, culture-minded Uticans were trickling into Mechanics Hall to view the Art Exhibition that was part of the Twentieth Annual Mechanics Association Fair. Two years later, the first formal Exhibition of Paintings and Sculpture offered by the newly formed Art Association included 283 *objets d'art.* These exhibitions were to continue to be a biennial part of the city's life; in 1878 Harold Frederic covered the sixth formal exhibition for his newspaper, the Utica *Observer.*[22]

Long before, however, during his first year at the Advanced School, he had solicited the judgment and advice of a local portrait painter, Arthur Pflanz, about one of his own sketches. Impressed with the boy's talent, Pflanz not only encouraged him, but actually taught him how to use oils. The fledgling artist promptly used his new skills to copy a portrait of Field Marshal von Moltke, whose career, for some lost reason, he was currently following.[23] Pflanz was his friend for life, and Frederic's interest in art continued long after he had abandoned any plans for a career as an artist.

Actually, however, Frederic probably had too little time for browsing in the Utica Library, looking at paintings in Mechanics Hall, or begging free art lessons from Arthur Pflanz. He still had his chores to do at home—the DeMott woodyard and dairy business was flourishing—and in 1871 there was more school work to do and examinations to prepare for if he planned to graduate from Advanced School and set out on his own. As it was, Harry Frederic could hardly have been the darling of his teachers. For one thing, he was too clever with colored chalk, and in caricatures on the walks near the schoolhouse the features of the Misses Skidmore, Brown, and Cook could be recognized too often for the artist's good. By now he had also begun to write stories during time that should have been devoted to other tasks. For refusing to surrender one of these stories to a teacher irritated by his inattention, Frederic later claimed, he was expelled from school.[24]

He may, indeed, have been suspended—the superintendent's annual reports show that suspension was a fairly common disciplinary measure—but he was certainly never expelled. For, during June, 1871, as the class fretted out the last month of school, he was busily rehearsing his role in the class play that was to be a part of the graduation exercises. During the first week of July, Frederic and his classmates suffered through their final ordeal, examinations. When they were completed, the name of "Harry H. Frederic" was safely on the list of sixty-one graduates; and the formal education of Harold Frederic was finished.[25]

CHAPTER 2

The Young Journalist, 1871-1884

FIFTEEN-YEAR-OLD Harold Frederic, his mother realized, had talents which hardly pointed in the direction of a career in the family's wood and milk business. Much as the business could have used the strength that Harry seemed to inherit from his Ramsdell forebears, the DeMotts apparently did not seriously hope to keep him in the barn or at the saw. His school days over, he was free to explore the city for more likely opportunities than their business presented.

After a series of odd jobs which Frederic himself never exactly recalled, he soon found one that he hoped was at least remotely attuned to his talents. This was in the studio of L. C. Mundy, Utica's most fashionable photographer, who specialized in photographic portraits "finished in India ink, crayon, oil, and water colors." Mundy's was a prosperous establishment with a reception room on the ground floor and processing-rooms upstairs in the studio at 11 Broad Street. If Frederic had dreams of quickly learning Mundy's professional secrets, he was disappointed. He was hired to run errands, to sweep the floor, and to tend the furnace; Mundy would let few of his employes, and certainly not a fifteen-year-old boy, into or even near his inner sanctum, the processing-room. After some weeks of performing menial tasks, the disillusioned boy searched for another, more interesting job.[1]

In the studio of a more indulgent photographer, A. C. Hopkins, he did learn to make commercial prints. After teaching him this simple skill, Hopkins was forced to fire Frederic for daydreaming and ruining a quantity of expensive paper. With still a third photographer, Abner B. Gardner, he was somewhat more successful. Under new tutelage, the chastened boy learned to retouch negatives—to remove unseemly warts, wrinkles, and blotches from the pictures of customers who wanted to look better than nature had ordained they should.[2] With Hopkins, Frederic acquired the technical knowledge of photography reflected in his later fiction, notably "Marsena," in which a minor character, the photographer's assistant, is a miniature self-portrait.

In August, 1872, with a number of boys who, like Frederic, had been too young to taste the glory of the war, he helped to form the Adjutant Bacon Corps of Cadets, an organization dedicated to wearing handsome uniforms and marching up and down Genesee Street with admirable precision during public functions. The group shrewdly ingratiated itself with the community by naming itself in memory of a local hero killed at the battle of Fredericksburg. With the area's friendly sponsorship assured, the Cadets were in great demand not only in Utica, but throughout the county and beyond. They met on Monday evenings to practice their intricate drills—including one done in blindfolds—in the Hutchison Building Armory on Bleecker Street. Grimly serious as they could be while their martinet leader, Captain Joseph O'Donnell, put them through their maneuvers, the Cadets were also socially-minded and capable of group pranks and of moments of organized levity. In 1873, Frederic, more skillful now than ever with his pencil, prepared an artful caricature of the club, superimposing photographs of members' faces over torsos drawn in various postures. Captain O'Donnell is shown riding a hobby-horse and carrying a club; Francis Kernan Baxter, Frederic's cousin, is pictured with bulging muscles and handling two other cadets effortlessly on his outstretched hands; Frederic shows himself, significantly, working at an easel.[3]

As Frederic's circle of acquaintance widened in the city, he also met in his home new and memorable people—memorable, even when they were not always so much fun as the Bacon Cadets. In April, 1873, for example, he met his first church dignitary, a real Methodist Bishop.

The week starting on Wednesday, April 16, was a busy one for Utica Methodists, for it marked the opening of the Northern New York Annual Conference, which was held in the new First Methodist Episcopal Church. For weeks, eager Methodists in Utica had been vying for the honor of lodging visiting church leaders in their homes during a conference seldom held in Utica. To the delight of Grandmother Ramsdell and Frances DeMott, the honor of providing quarters for the most important visitors of all—the august Bishop Jesse Truesdell Peck and his wife—fell to the roomy, well-situated DeMott home.[4] Although this was his first official episcopal visit to Utica, Bishop Peck was well known and admired in Utica and, indeed, throughout the East. Uticans remembered that Peck had delivered the evening sermon on the day the new First ME Church was dedicated in 1871; now he was back again as a bishop, and old acquaintances wanted to pay their respects.

Harold Frederic could hardly have known, of course, that the kind, elderly Bishop and his wife who roomed in his home during the conference had an infant grandnephew in Newark, New Jersey, named Stephen Crane, who was later to figure in Frederic's own life. Perhaps as a busy teenage boy he even found ways to avoid exchanging words with Bishop and Mrs. Peck, although this seems doubtful. In any case, he must have been part of the congregation in the First Methodist Episcopal Church at the final session of the Conference on Tuesday, May 22, when Bishop Peck read the list of new pastoral appointments and then spoke "very feelingly in regard to the burden that had been on his mind, touching [the] various appointments."[5] Frederic was to remember the scene vividly as he wrote the opening chapter of *The Damnation of Theron Ware* more than twenty years afterwards. But whether Stephen Crane, who became his friend later, ever recognized his own granduncle in Frederic's picture of the "slow, near-sighted old gentleman" who starts Theron Ware on his way to doom will probably never be known.

I

Even with its various kinds of appeal, however, the job at the photographer's, the occasional exciting political campaigns, the high-jinks of the congenial Bacon Cadets, and the infrequent but impressing appearance of some very important ecclesiastical personage like Bishop Peck, Utica was still a small town in 1873 and a seventeen-year-old boy wished to expand his horizons. Sometime during the late spring or early summer of 1873, in the middle of one of the worst depressions in American history, Frederic either left or lost his latest job, said good-bye to his family and friends, and boarded an east-bound train for Boston.

His choice of this "big city" was entirely natural. To any young man with even a dim dream of an artistic or literary career, Boston was still a Mecca in 1873; and Harold Frederic was neither the first nor last to make the holy journey. Thirteen years before, William Dean Howells, another young man from a farther West than Frederic's, had established the pattern and had grown in little more than a decade from country boy to editor of the mighty *Atlantic Monthly.* Eleven years later, in 1884, Hamlin Garland, who traveled an even longer distance from South Dakota, aimed at Harvard College but was willing to settle for the Boston Public Library.

But Frederic at seventeen was no young Howells intent on meeting and learning from the Cambridge and Concord prophets. There was no New England idolatry in his heart, now or later. If he ever so much as saw, even at a distance on Boston streets, any of the Brahmins—men like Emerson, Lowell, and Holmes, whose doorsteps the worshipful Howells had haunted in 1860—Frederic never mentioned the event. He regarded Boston as a city which might find use for his talents in a year when jobs were scarce. And even when he did find work as a retoucher for the photography firm of Rowell and Allen, he spent his leisure time not in seeking out America's intellectual and literary giants, but in roaming the Common, two blocks south of his rooming house on Staniford Street; in loitering on Saturday nights in a billiard "academy"; and in visiting art galleries where he admired pictures and portraits that would never hang in Mechanics' Hall back in Utica. Occasionally he wrote to Pflanz, urging him to bring his paints and brushes to the city. He bought books, too, especially the novels of Erckmann-Chatrian, which he continued to read with delight even in the shadow of the capital of a more sophisticated literary world.[6]

Frederic did not know, of course, that in his *Atlantic Monthly* offices editor William Dean Howells was hammering out a set of literary principles that would command at least the partial allegiance of a generation of American novelists including Frederic himself. In the twenty-some months that he spent in Boston, Frederic possibly may never have heard of Howells, much less have known him or his columns about the new realism. Three years later, when he had written the first fiction he judged worthy of publication, the idea of sending it to *The Atlantic* apparently did not occur to him.

For Frederic was never to be a Bostonian, proper or otherwise; and, by the summer of 1875, he had left the Brahmin capital to return to Utica. Perhaps he had met too many men like Miles Arbuton and Staniford—characters whom Howells created as indictments of proper Boston in the early 1870's. Perhaps he had lost his job with Rowell and Allen; or perhaps he was merely homesick for the Mohawk Valley. Whatever the reason for his return, Frederic carried back with him no reverence for New England or its traditions. Later, and for the rest of his life both as journalist and novelist, he was to allow himself the occasional pleasure of digs at what he called "Boston talkers."[7]

But the experience at least supplied him with a store of anecdotes and worldly observations with which he could impress his fellow Bacon Cadets who had never seen Boston. Affecting a long-tailed frock coat and hinting at his knowledge of artists' life in great cities, Frederic once more went to work for the Utica photographer, Mundy—but not for long. There were more interesting things to do for a living, even in Utica, than retouching photographs. Realizing that working with words can be as exciting as working with brushes, he had begun to write stories. A whole new world, he discovered, was open to those who know what words are for. Late in the summer of 1875 he left Mundy's permanently to begin work as a proofreader for the Utica *Morning Herald* at the substantial salary of twelve dollars a week.[8]

The *Herald*, one of Utica's two daily papers, was vigorously Republican. Harold Frederic, already a thoroughgoing young Democrat, could hardly have felt completely at home on its staff. But his job on the *Herald* served only as a starting point; after only a few weeks, Frederic decided that he did not care to work nights, as he was required to do for a morning newspaper. When a new opportunity occurred as proofreader for the other daily, the Utica *Observer,* he quickly accepted it. The *Observer* was an afternoon paper, and as vigorously Democratic as the *Herald* was Republican. Frederic was happy to change jobs for more reasons than one.

The *Observer,* with a history dating from 1816, had in 1875 a daily circulation of over 3,000 which was somewhat less than that claimed by its morning competitor.[9] The *Observer* was owned and operated by a trio of journalistic and political veterans—DeWitt C. Grove, Elijah Prentiss Bailey, and Theodore Pease Cook; and each of them had much to teach the new proofreader who had joined their interesting company. All three were active Democrats. Grove, who had been mayor of Utica from 1860 through 1862, was a constant critic of Senator Roscoe Conkling and his faction. Bailey, son of a fighting Abolitionist editor and a printer since he was twelve, now ruled the pressroom with benevolent authority. Cook, thirty-one years old and the youngest of the three, was also the most brilliant and articulate. A graduate of Columbia Law School, he was a fiery-penned reformer who took the excesses of the Grant administration as a series of personal insults. His hopes for the future of America were solidly pinned on New York's Governor Samuel J. Tilden, whose presidential campaign biography he was planning to write when the time came. These men, with a few subordinates and the inevitable tramp printers, taught Harold Frederic his first lessons in journalism.

Hired as a proofreader, Frederic soon had opportunities to perform more interesting tasks. On a medium-sized daily like the *Observer,* no staff member stayed at the same job for long; before and after the proof was read, there were numerous small editorial chores to do and Frederic learned quickly to do them. In an editorial office much like the one that figures so prominently in *Seth's Brother's Wife,* he learned to watch the wire, for instance, for stories of state, national, and even international affairs; how to spot, clip, and paste up for reprinting in the *Observer* especially interesting or pointed items from New York and Boston papers; and best of all, perhaps, how to keep in firm touch with goings-on in Utica itself.

For the city had grown now to a healthy 35,000. Life

floated in and out on two canals, the Chenango as well as the Erie, which met sluggishly only a few blocks from the *Observer* office. Four railroad lines brought people, goods, and more life to the city. Six temperance and as many musical societies welcomed notices of any kind in the *Observer*—or, for that matter, in any of the eighteen different publications, including a Welsh and a German newspaper, that flourished in Utica.[10] And the city was now even more politically minded than ever, especially after the 1875 elections, which sent Francis Kernan, a highly respected Utica Democrat, to the United States Senate. Since Roscoe Conkling was already there, the State of New York was now represented in the upper house by a pair of Uticans who lived only blocks from each other. Other American cities, Frederic's townsmen liked to point out, might be happy to have *one* Senator: only Utica had two.

Thriving on the constant demands of his unfolding new career and apparently avoiding the pitfalls that he was later to set in the way of the young hero of *Seth's Brother's Wife,* Harry Frederic, as Uticans still knew him, was now a promising young man about town. He still lived at home, where his mother, stepfather, and grandmother undoubtedly watched him with pride. In young-man fashion, he prowled the city with his old friends of the Bacon Cadets, his younger Baxter cousins, and artist Arthur Pflanz. Whatever they thought of Frederic's affectations—the frockcoat draped on his stooping, six-foot frame; the mustache, goatee, and longish hair; and the frequent reminiscences about Bohemian life in Boston—these old friends stayed with him, and he with them.

To some of them, perhaps, he confided the ambition that by now was beginning to boil within him: to be a writer. For by early 1876, the die was certainly cast and Frederic was trying his hand at sustained fiction which, although it could not be marketed, was at least worth preserving. The first such effort, written possibly as early as 1874, when he was in Boston, was entitled "The Jew's Christmas." Like the early work of many writers, this story suffers from sentimentality: it tells of an aged, scholarly Jew who buys presents and a Christmas tree for a little Christian girl and later adopts her.[11] Whether or not Frederic ever tried to find a publisher for the story is not known; the fact that he carefully saved it, however, is significant.

By May, 1876, he had finished another work, almost 12,000 words in length, entitled "The Story of Peter Zarl." Whatever he may have thought of the worth of "The Jew's Christmas," his regard for "Peter Zarl" is a matter of his own record. "Completed copy May 12, '76," he wrote neatly in the corner of a blank title-page; then, "mailed Harper's June 1, '76; mailed Lippincott's July 31, '76; mailed Leslie's Nov. 20, '76." The manuscript itself is liberally corrected; Frederic must have tried after each rejection to improve his story before sending it out again.[12] His efforts were futile; for the story was never published—probably because the editors recognized it as an amateurish and overt imitation of the Erckmann-Chatrian tone and formula. Disappointed as he must have been with the story's failure, Frederic possibly learned an important lesson from "Peter Zarl"; in any case, his next one and the first to appear in print, was set not in Erckmann-Chatrian's Alsace (as is "Peter Zarl") but in his own Mohawk Valley.

On June 30, 1877, the Utica *Observer* published "The Blakelys of Poplar Place. A Legend of the Mohawk"; and Harold Frederic was off to a modest start as a writer of fiction. Still redolent in places of the historical romances, "The Blakelys of Poplar Place" nevertheless represents a long step forward in Frederic's development as a writer. Set against the Revolution as it was fought in the Mohawk Valley—that is, against the bloody split between Valley Tories and Valley patriots—"The Blakelys of Poplar Place" anticipates in a number of ways the later novel, *In the Valley*. Melodramatic and mechanical in too many places, the story shows less dependence on models than anything he had yet written; and it indicates that Frederic was already capable of inventing his own devices. Anyway, the editors of his paper liked it; and Harry Frederic had reason to be pleased with this first published product of his imagination.

II

As he worked his way from proofreader to reporter for the *Observer* and dreamed of more success as a writer of fiction, Frederic was developing in still other ways. As a newspaperman he was concerned with the present—with what was happening at the moment in and around a small city enveloped in the Gilded Age. But he was also becoming increasingly conscious of the past from which his own society had evolved. Early in 1877 he became a charter member of the Oneida Historical Society,[13] an organization which planned as its first important undertaking the centennial of the battle of Oriskany. An omnivorous reader of history ever since his first encounter with books, Frederic had long been fascinated by the social implications behind this bloody skirmish which had been fought on a rolling slope only seven miles from his birthplace. Sometime in 1875 or 1876, he had read Williams L. Stone's well-known *Life of Joseph Brant* and had been impressed by Stone's vivid, well-documented account of Oriskany. Now, with the centennial of the battle some months in the offing, he wrote, with an enthusiasm more vigorous than innocent, what amounted to a paraphrase of whole sections of Stone's work, expanding or shortening passages as he saw fit. This slightly modified version of Stone's account Frederic sent under his own title, "The Mohawk Valley During the Revolution," to *Harper's New Monthly.* Accepted by an unsuspecting editor, the article appeared in the July issue.[14] Frederic's first appearance before the larger world and in a reputable publication was marked with something less than honor.

Both Utica newspapers noted the publication of Frederic's article in *Harper's.* His own paper, the *Observer,* proudly reprinted the long concluding section describing the battle;[15] the opposition paper, the *Herald,* sternly accused the young author of plagiarism and hinted broadly that this was reprehensible chicanery to be expected from the *Observer* staff. Frederic, then or later, said nothing. But perhaps one of his more experienced acquaintances pointed out to him that what was common practice in the newspaper world was considered unethical in other quarters. In any case, nobody except the editors of the *Herald* seemed upset.

Meanwhile, the infant Oneida Historical Society had persisted with its plans; and the Oriskany Centennial celebration on a sunny August 6, 1877, was, as Frederic recalled later, "a marked success" which had attracted a huge crowd. "People flocked by uncounted thousands to the historic ground," wrote one eye-witness. "They came from all parts of the State, and those of the Mohawk Valley, in particular, turned out *en masse*."[16] As one present suggested later, "It was probably the largest gathering ever seen in the State, outside one or two of the larger cities."

One of the speakers of the day was Frederic's old idol, ex-Governor Horatio Seymour. Like another John Quincy Adams, Seymour was still serving the people who had sent him to high places and rounding out his days in a minor office as supervisor of roads in his own town of Deerfield, a part of Utica. The great audience at Oriskany listened to him carefully that day as he delivered his usual intelligent address—and one in which he called for familiarity with area history as a step toward closer national unity. "Historians have done much, and well," he told the crowd that covered the field, "in making up the records of the past. But their recitals have not yet become, as they should be, a part of the general intelligence of our people." The people, he went on, simply did not know enough about the part New York had played in shaping the nation. "There is a dimness in the popular vision," he pointed out, "about this great centre, source, and theatre of events which have shaped the civilization, usages, and government of this continent. This is not only a wrong to our State but to our Union."

To him neglect of New York history had resulted in an incomplete understanding of national history: "it has left the annals of other sections disjointed from their true relationships to the great body of our traditions."[17] With these careful words, Seymour was actually voicing an old New York complaint: that New England, having produced popular historians, was taking more than her share of credit for American history itself. But he was also proposing that New Yorkers could set things straight by investigating their own past—one that had to be understood before national history could be properly written.

Somewhere in the immense crowd listening to Seymour stood young Harold Frederic, busily taking notes for his newspaper story and wondering, perhaps, how one could best make a distant historical event (like the battle of Oriskany, for example) "part of the general intelligence of our people."

Seymour's attitude toward local and area history, and his insistence that it can be seen in "due proportion" and "proper perspective" as part of national history, had an immediate and lasting effect on Frederic. "It was at this time," he recalled later, "that I gathered the first materials for my projected work."[18] The "projected work" was *In the Valley*, which was to simmer in his mind for over a decade before it finally appeared in 1890, with a dedication to the memory of "a venerable friend, to whose inspiration my first idea of the work was due . . . the foremost citizen of New York State, Horatio Seymour."

Altogether, 1877, his twenty-first year, was an eventful one for Harold Frederic. It had seen the publication of his first successful story and the appearance in a national magazine, however questionable the circumstances, of his first article. The centennial, with all its color and excitement, and especially Seymour's provocative address had provided him with a plan for the future: he would write a full-scale novel, a *magnum opus* worthy of the dramatic history of the Mohawk Valley. Truly, Frederic could have reflected in August, this had been a big year; but it was not over yet: the most important event of all was still to occur.

Two months after the Oriskany Centennial, on October 10, 1877, Frederic married Grace Williams, a Utica girl whom he had probably known most of his life. Slender and delicate, with remarkably beautiful eyes, Grace had lived only a block from the DeMott home for several years; and presumably she had watched with deep interest the rising fortunes of the tall, hearty young newspaperman. Grace's mother, Ruth Williams, also saw promise in Harry Frederic—even more, perhaps, than her daughter did.

In rapidly failing health, Ruth Williams was anxious to see her quiet daughter safely married before she herself died. Ruth—the daughter of Beriah Green, the old Whitesboro firebrand who had stirred the state with his militant abolitionism thirty years before—had been indoctrinated with a belief in the holy efficacy of early marriage. As Ruth's end drew near, certain arrangements were made for the culmination of what actually had been a rather restrained romance. Frederic and Grace were married at what proved to be the deathbed of the bride's mother—a detail which appeared later in the description of the marriage of Theron and Alice in *The Damnation of Theron Ware.* But, in spite of the depressing circumstances surrounding the wedding, there was little unhappiness in sight as yet. Frederic's affable mother welcomed the young couple into the roomy DeMott house, where they remained until spring before moving into their own home at 58 Mary Street.

III

Meanwhile, Frederic's abilities continued to develop, and his work on the *Observer* soon carried him to all corners of the city and county. By 1878 he was a seasoned reporter, entrusted with important assignments that took him, for instance, to a sensational murder case in Chenango County, where he came face to face with a "rural murderer" much like Milton Squires of *Seth's Brother's Wife.*[19] He learned also from his excursions into county courtrooms that farm life in upstate New York could be a pretty grim business and one altogether different from the pleasantly bustling life in the small but comfortable city of Utica. Exciting as his traveling assignments were, Frederic undoubtedly felt more at ease in Utica. And so, in May, 1879, when he was promoted to news editor of the *Observer,* a post that kept him close to the city's hum and buzz, he had several reasons to be pleased. There were always new people and occasionally new ideas to be met in Utica; and they were easier to find when one was an editor and not a mere reporter.

As early as 1877 Frederic came in contact with a variety of stimulating ideas through one of the new people: Father Edward A. Terry, a priest recently assigned to St. John's Church, the spiritual headquarters of most of Utica's large Irish-Catholic population. Father Terry, born in Ireland, was familiar with intellectual concepts that were strange not only to Frederic but to the vast majority of his own parishioners as well. A big, broad-faced, handsome, eloquent Irishman, Father Terry had won the love of his people soon after his arrival in Utica in 1876. Most of his parishioners were unaware of Father Terry's "liberal" theology; they were happy that they had a priest, an Irishman like themselves, who could match the pulpit oratory of any minister in the county and, moreover, one who would charter whole trains to take them, on occasion, to boisterous parish picnics at Trenton Falls.[20] In fact, few Utica Catholics of the 1870's would have wondered about the theology of an ordained priest; and, indeed, there is little evidence that Father Terry gave his parishioners any serious cause to wonder. But, in the quiet atmosphere of a private home and to a pleasant, intellectually curious young Protestant like Frederic, the priest was probably more candid and revelatory than he had occasion to be before his assembled congregation.

In private, Father Terry could, and undoubtedly did, talk like Father Forbes, the modernist priest of *The Damnation of Theron Ware.* His apparently casual attitude toward what, in Frederic's staunchly Methodist home, had always been cherished as "sacred truths" was hardly as shocking or unorthodox as it must have seemed to Frederic; it was simply an attitude toward religion and religious mystery that he had not met before and that he was doubly surprised to find in a Roman Catholic priest. Father Terry did little to discourage the friendship. He and Frederic met frequently and most often at the home of Thomas McQuade, who had two daughters. One, Josephine, had beautiful red hair; the other, Catherine, loved to play Chopin on the McQuade piano; Frederic combined these details later in the character of Celia Madden, the striking aesthetic organist in *Theron Ware.* Altogether, young Frederic gained immeasurably from his acquaintance with Father Terry, just as he had profited from his admiration for Seymour. Just as Seymour had given him an attitude toward history, so did the brilliant priest give him an attitude toward religion—not by trying to entice him to Catholicism but by calmly opening for him new paths to intellectual excitement of which Frederic had never dreamed.

Frederic's admiration for the priest's mind and talents were soon revealed in the *Observer.* In June and July, 1879, shortly after Frederic became news editor, the paper printed on its front pages a series of particularly effective sermons that Father Terry was delivering at St. John's. One of these was a reasoned reply to a Presbyterian charge that the Roman Catholic Church was not a Christian church. "We make no apology," wrote Frederic in introducing the text of the sermon, "for surrendering so much of our space today to the second sermon."[21] And in March, 1880, when Father Terry was invited by a citizens' committee to address the people of Utica about the current plight of Ireland, Frederic heard and applauded the speech. Once more he wrote, on March 17, 1880, "We make no apology for giving [the address] the large space it occupies in today's *Observer*. But happy they who heard it warm from the speaker's lips and who have not to content themselves with the lesser pleasure of reading it."

But interesting as Frederic found the priest's public defenses of Catholicism and his highly colored appeals for help for famine-ridden Ireland, it was Father Terry's occasional explication of doctrine in historical terms that most intrigued him. On Sunday, May 2, 1880, Frederic attended an evening service at St. John's. "Father Terry's address explaining the service," he wrote in the following day's *Observer*, "was replete with information touching the origin of the Christian Church, which he traced from the Pagan inceptions through the first adoption by the early church as a means of drawing the people into the true fold by humoring their habits and customs, until they were finally transformed into devout ceremonies, thoroughly imbued with the spirit of Christianity. Father Terry explained that the devotion to the month of May in the Catholic Church was originally a dedication by the Pagans to the Goddess of Maya, the representative of the idea of maternity. . . . Father Terry explained incidentally the nomenclature of months and seasons which has come down to us from Pagan times, and his sermon throughout was not only characteristically eloquent, but was filled with the most interesting information."[22] Fifteen years later, the Reverend Theron Ware was to be disturbed by the "interesting information" coming from a Roman Catholic priest; but his creator, Harold Frederic, had found it most stimulating.

As he talked with Father Terry in private, listened to his sermons, and watched him at his sacred offices, Frederic gained new insight into the sociological and the religious workings of his society. Until recently, he had seen these parishioners of St. John's as benighted and alien Irish—sons and grandsons of shiploads of ignorant canal-diggers who, as such, were hardly worth consideration as *bona fide* citizens. Frederic, descended from settlers who had been old residents of the valley before the city of Utica was even born, began to look differently at these newcomers of whom Father Terry was so fond and who so loved him. After all, the Irish had produced Edward Aloysius Terry—and undoubtedly more like him. If this sophisticated, erudite, and personable priest were a representative of what the Irish could produce in a single generation, they should be recognized for what they were: a potentially powerful social and moral force in America. From his friendship with Father Terry stemmed, therefore, not only Frederic's interest in the history of religion but also his interest in the Irish as a people—an interest that was to influence much of his later life and work.

IV

In May, 1880, when Theodore P. Cook suddenly abandoned his post as editor of the *Observer,* twenty-four-year-old Harold Frederic was appointed his successor. The promotion meant, first of all, an increase in salary that Frederic could well use; for Grace had presented him with a daughter, Ruth, in 1878, and another child was on the way. But besides keeping him closer to the office the new responsibilities cut shorter than ever the hours he had once been able to devote to the writing of fiction. Since becoming news editor early in 1879, he had produced only one story, which the *Observer* had printed on September 6, 1879—"Brother Sebastian's Friendship," another romantic tale with an incredible plot and too many echoes still of Erckmann-Chatrian.

The exalted new post was not particularly exciting. After the relatively desultory presidential campaign of 1880 (Frederic and the *Observer* could not muster much enthusiasm for the Democratic candidate, Winfield Scott Hancock), things were generally quiet in Utica. Even Father Terry was mysteriously transferred by his bishop in September, 1880, to St. Ann's, in Albany, much to the open annoyance of his Utica congregation. Frederic did what he could to forestall the transfer; for, as early as April, when a rumor swept Utica that the good priest had antagonized other area clergy with his daring sermons and was to be rusticated, Frederic had written: "it is not easy to believe that the Bishop . . . will take Father Terry from Utica. That honored prelate . . . cannot but have caught a reflection of the love and respect with which the young priest is held here. . . . Thousands will join the *Observer* in the hopeful prayer that he may be retained here, where he has done so much that is good."[23] But five months later the blow fell, and the people of St. John's bade farewell to the "darling priest" with muttered protests for which Father Terry rebuked them in his final sermon entitled "Catholic Obedience."[24]

The loss of his stimulating friend did little to allay the restlessness that Frederic felt during the following two years. There was much activity in the city, of course, but it was routine; and Frederic was never to adapt readily to routine of any kind. His days were filled with observing and commenting on minor political squabbles and local events which had lost savor for a man who had grown in Frederic's direction. Roscoe Conkling was always there to attack, and Frederic allowed himself the regular luxury of striking out at the Republican stalwart whose political star was then on the wane. But Frederic's old zest seemed gone.

In June, 1882, Frederic's editorial attention returned for a time to a subject Father Terry had so vividly dramatized in his speech to the people of Utica: the Irish troubles. When Michael Davitt, the Irish patriot, landed in New York to preach his views on the Irish question, Frederic followed his tour with interest. In a series of comments in the *Observer* during June and July, furthermore, he demonstrated not only his interest in the subject, but also a remarkable grasp of the intricate distinction between Davitt's plan for Irish land relief and Parnell's.[25] Already he was preparing himself for international tasks that he did not dream were so near in the future.

At the age of twenty-four, Frederic had gone as far as he could in Utica; the time had come for him to move; and the opportunity came suddenly and unexpectedly. In August, 1882, he was offered the editorship of the Albany *Evening Journal.* Properly flattered, for the *Journal* was a more influential paper than the *Observer,* Frederic accepted the post and wondered about a home in Albany for Grace and their two daughters. Finally deciding to leave his family in Utica until a suitable house could be found, he boarded a train on August 31 for the mother city of the Mohawk Valley.[26]

The new editor, twenty-six years old now, apparently went to his new assignment with few misgivings about political complications. Frederic's entire journalistic experience, except for his few weeks with the *Herald*, had been with the Democratic Utica *Observer;* the Albany *Journal*, although it was a "half-breed"—that is, an anti-Conkling—paper, was nevertheless staunchly Republican. Since its foundation in 1830 by Thurlow Weed, unofficial leader first of New York Whigs and later of its Republicans, the *Journal* had been one of the most influential organs of what to Frederic was "the other side." Intent on getting a closer view of state politics, he refused, however, to let his own partisan convictions interfere with his career. But some kind of trouble was inevitable, and it came quickly—before Frederic had been a month in Albany.

In September, 1882, the Republican State Convention at Saratoga nominated Charles J. Folger for governor. Folger, currently serving as President Arthur's Secretary of the Treasury, was hardly the candidate to unite the state Republican party which had been split since 1880 as the result of a feud between President Garfield and Roscoe Conkling. Folger's nomination for governor not only enraged the already unhappy reform elements within the Republican organization but widened the split.

Fresh at his new desk as editor of the most influential Republican newspaper in upstate New York, Harold Frederic welcomed the opportunity to carry over an enmity he had acquired from DeWitt C. Grove and the Utica *Observer* and to wage big-time war on Conkling. On September 21, 1882, the Albany *Evening Journal* announced in Frederic's editorial that it had irrevocably bolted the Saratoga ticket that Conkling supported. As was customary, dozens of local Republican papers throughout the State followed the *Journal's* (or Frederic's) lead; and Folger's defeat was certain. At the polls in November, New York State overwhelmingly elected as its new governor the hitherto little-known "veto mayor" of Buffalo, Grover Cleveland; and the maverick editor of the quondam orthodox Republican *Evening Journal* found a new Democratic idol to replace the forgotten Tilden and the aging Seymour.

The new governor, forthright and independent, went at his task with vigor; and the supposedly Republican *Journal*, which had never openly endorsed Cleveland except by refusing to support his opponent, became noticeably uncritical of an opposition administration. The editor was not long in making himself known personally to the Governor, and they soon became good friends. "Frederic often dropped into the governor's office," says Allan Nevins, Cleveland's biographer, "and gradually developed an enthusiastic admiration for Cleveland. It repeatedly cropped out in supposedly Republican editorials of the *Evening Journal* like veins of gold in a cold quartz ledge."[27] In turn, says Nevins, "Frederic's wit and cultivation appealed to Cleveland as a welcome change from the shoals of politicians. . . . Versatile, light-hearted, full of ideas, [Frederic's] talk diverted the Governor, while his editorials were among the few which Cleveland read."

Grover Cleveland, although the highest-placed, was not the only new friend to be attracted by Frederic's "wit and cultivation." Edgar Kelsey Apgar, the tiny, brilliant Deputy State Treasurer who had masterminded Cleveland's election,[28] was also among his familiars. "I recall not less than a hundred conversations with him over our little dinner table," wrote Frederic later.[29] Apgar was "very proud of being a politician, pure and simple, and protested vehemently against the popular tendency to decry the professional politician as an element not to be encouraged."[30] The fiery intensity of this little man—"his weight was ordinarily about one hundred pounds"[31]—and his complete dedication to honesty in the Democratic party amused Frederic even as it inspired him. Much of what he learned from Apgar appeared later in *Seth's Brother's Wife* not only in the idealist-reformer Richard Ansdell but also in the honest political boss, Abe Beekman.

With his eye on political developments all over the state, Frederic continued to applaud Cleveland's strokes for sound government. On April 10, 1883, after Cleveland had vetoed a Democrat-sponsored bill designed to dismember the efficient Buffalo fire department, the *Journal* had high editorial praise:

"If the Bourbon Democracy made a mistake last November," Frederic wrote, alluding to the fact that Grover Cleveland had been a compromise candidate, "the people didn't. Grover Cleveland has shown himself what we took him on trust to be last fall—bigger and better than his party." And finally, less than a month later, on May 11, Frederic boldly suggested that in Cleveland the Democrats had an admirable and deserving candidate for the presidency. Before this suggestion caught on, however, and was ultimately acted upon in the Democratic Convention which nominated Cleveland more than a year later, Frederic's whole life had changed.

In March, 1884, the Republican *Journal,* with whose politics Frederic had so freely tampered, was suddenly sold. The new owner had his own plans for the paper, and Frederic was not included in them: the close friend of the next president of the United States was out of a job. Angry and hurt at being "broken on the wheel," as he later called it, Frederic was convinced that he was being punished for his public admiration of an honest Democratic governor. With no regrets, however, he now paused briefly to consider the next step, in what had been, up to this point, a promising career. Two alternatives seemed open to him: he could go back to Utica and the *Observer,* which could always make good use of his widening vision. Or he could gamble on something bigger than a lifetime post on a small city daily which would give him security but probably little else.

Frederic chose to gamble. With a recommendation from the sympathetic and influential Apgar, he was soon negotiating with the New York *Times,* which needed a foreign correspondent. Early in June he joined the *Times* staff and was immediately assigned to the London office; his job was "to summarize, in perspective, to add relevant details, to weigh public opinion, and thus to interpret" events in England and on the continent. "He was to cable his stories home, once or twice a week, depending on their urgency; his salary was to be $80 a week."[32] With an entirely new kind of life before him, he sailed with his family—Grace and the two daughters, Ruth and Ruby—on the *Queen* on June 11, 1884.

CHAPTER 3

Foreign Correspondent and Author, 1884-1898

WHEN THE young journalist shepherded his family from the ship at Southampton onto a London-bound train, he was only twenty-eight. In some respects he was mature beyond his years; in others, he was a fledgling, raw and underdeveloped for the sophisticated society into which he was about to fly. Before boarding the ship in New York, he had gone to *Times* Editor Edward P. Mitchell not to discover what his duties in London would be but to learn what tips he was expected to pay aboard ship to table and room stewards. Having given him some inexpert advice, Mr. Mitchell waved farewell and watched the young man lumber awkwardly out the door in "a long green overcoat that made him look like a cucumber."[1]

If Frederic took stock of his assets, after he had reached England, these might well have caused an older man than he to smile with pride. The *Observer* and *Journal* years were behind him now, but the richness of experience that he had gained was to be of good use. He had left his many American friends, but the memory of them was comforting; and their counsel was to serve him, whether or not he ever acknowledged it with more than a grunt of approval or dismissal. He had a good position on one of the greatest of American newspapers and a salary that, as he looked back to the day when he had lost his post on the Albany paper, surely was larger than he had dreamed of getting. He may have wondered whether he had been wise to reject so flatly Grover Cleveland's appeal for him to enter politics—on the ground that the political game was a dirty one.[2] But in his pocket he had the Governor's letter:

> Mr. Harold Frederic until recently was a resident of the city of Albany, where I have enjoyed this acquaintance and friendship.
>
> His ability and success as a journalist are conceded; and I am much pleased to have the opportunity of testifying to his rare attainments, as well as to his qualities of heart and mind, that have made him my friend and gained for him an enviable place in the estimation of the entire community.
>
> /s/ Grover Cleveland
> GOVERNOR OF THE STATE OF NEW YORK
>
> ATTEST: /s/ Daniel S. Lamont
> Private Secretary[3]

He must have shown this letter to Grace with pride, and it must have given him assurance as he faced London!

For the moment, however, he had to be concerned with Grace and his two little daughters as their train puffed its way northward and eastward, through Hampshire and Surrey, and at length pulled into Waterloo Station. If he experienced a brief hesitancy there, in the confusion of the smoke-filled shed, in the chatter of high-pitched voices speaking a language almost foreign to him, in the cries of the cabbies and the swirl of passengers, he soon recovered his self-confidence and aplomb.

Within three short weeks, as he wrote to his editor, Charles R. Miller, he had established his office at 203 Strand, West Central London, and had ensconced his family in a "fine house in Bayswater," where he thought Mrs. Frederic, who had been ill, and the two little girls, who had whooping cough, might "recover health and spirits."[4] Meanwhile, he discovered London and met as many people as he could. Thereafter he set about writing dispatches to his paper, a duty in which he was not to falter in the fourteen years of life that remained to him.

I

Even in the first of these dispatches, Frederic revealed the firmness of his experienced hand. There was to be no fumbling in his work for the *Times*. By July 13, not even a month after his arrival in London, he was on the way to becoming one of the truly great correspondents of the New York paper. Fortuitously for him but tragically for thousands of people in southern France, a cholera epidemic broke out in Toulon; and, though Frederic tried to find someone to go to the plague-stricken area to get firsthand details, he met only determined refusals and finally went himself.

One may read his weekly reports of the plague to the *Times*, beginning with the issue of July 27, 1884, and continuing through August 24 of that year—but occasional references to it appeared even later. He spent five days in Marseilles, Toulon, and Arles, where the epidemic reached its greatest proportions. He walked or rode through the streets, visited patients in hospitals, and witnessed the horror of a mass burial of plague victims in a night-time funeral that lacked all ceremony but a priest's consecration. With no more than a sizeable piece of cut plug in his mouth to serve as a preventive and with his usual buoyant good health, Frederic took very real risks to get his story, "Down Among the Dead Men."

"My conclusion," he wrote in this first article, "is that the much-dreaded cholera, probably the most fatal of all diseases to which human flesh is heir, is a thing of which no intelligent community of well-ordered lives and well-managed sewer pipes need have an alarming fear, even when brought into close contact with it. . . ."[5] With these reassuring words, he allayed the fears of people in England and elsewhere who in some cases had become almost hysterical. But he had learned the shocking and, to him, almost unbelievable disparity between the poor in his own country and the downtrodden masses of Europe: between the relative cleanliness of the cities and towns in his native New York and the filthy, disease-rotted quarters of the Old World. As a reporter, he had learned to face the hard realities of squalor in the Mohawk Valley; but what he saw in Toulon and Arles surpassed what even the most morbid American mind might conceive.

Returning to London, he was soon to see his report widely circulated and reprinted and his courageous adventure in southern France bring him a reputation for his action which was regarded as heroic.[6] English and French as well as

American papers acclaimed him. His career as a foreign correspondent was succcessfully begun. Probably no other act on his part could have brought him so quickly before the British public nor won for him so handily the respect and admiration of his colleagues of the press.

But if the honor coming to him for his articles on the cholera epidemic was not enough to recommend him to English readers, his portrait of Grover Cleveland as the new president, published in the *Pall Mall Gazette* following the November election, impressed them. Frederic took the liberty of quoting directly from a personal letter that he had received from Cleveland; then, thinking that perhaps he had overstepped the proper bounds in doing so, he wrote the President on November 8, 1884:

> I have first of all to express to you my fear that you will be vexed with me at having published in my *Pall Mall Gazette* article a part of the kind and manly letter you sent me the other day. But the temptation to let these English people have a reason for the faith that is in me, fresh from your own hand, was to [*sic*] strong to be resisted. . . . If I did you wrong, you will know how to forgive the act for the sake of the spirit in which it was committed.[7]

Unquestionably Frederic impulsively took this liberty and it can not be credited as opportunism on his part. For, as the letter continues, Frederic's awareness of affairs in his own country, his enthusiastic idealism, his buoyancy of spirit, and yet his ability also to face realities are all apparent. "Truly, my friend," he wrote,

> I think I realize now for the first time that stalwart pride, as of the ancient Roman citizenship, which the Clays and Bentons and Jacksons of past generations felt in their birthright of a whole continent, and which we of a punier growth, smarting under foreign criticism, aping foreign customs, seeking in the race for dishonored wealth to win class distinction and the idleness of the aristocrat in older countries, had almost completely lost. So long had I seen and hated these modern tendencies in our people; so trivial and selfish and unworthy had seemed to me the aims and ends for which Americans worked, the gods before which they did fetish worship, and the political harangues by which

> they justified themselves, that I may be said to have grown up with more indignation at, than pride in, my country and my countrymen. In my little way, I have tried to set things right—and you know how I was broken on the wheel for it. . . .

Some of this letter, no doubt, may be regarded as language running away with Frederic, some of it as over-fine writing. Yet Frederic never sank to the level of journalese; and, as his early dispatches to the *Times* reveal, he had a fondness for the well-managed sentence and for the precise word. In this Cleveland letter, as in many others to the President and sundry friends, Frederic's knowledge of history is apparent; and his understanding of the tragic era of the Grant administration and after—as one regards it from the vantage point of a century's perspective—makes him seem more remarkable still. His impetuousness, his ardor, his enthusiasm: these were the very qualities of character that won him friends in London. That so young a man could be an intimate of the President of the United States, as Cleveland's letter made plain, was sufficient for taking the *Times* correspondent seriously.

A third event significant to Frederic early in his London days was his achieving membership in the Savage Club. Pressing his English friend, Aaron Watson, who was also a newspaper man, he managed to be elected to membership before he had been in England more than eight months. Watson, telling the story in his *A Newspaper Man's Memories,* indicates that it was a matter of "some delicacy" because of Frederic's recent appearance in London; but, because of his background in newspaper work and Cleveland's letter of recommendation, he was accepted.[8] Then, hoping that the New York *Times* would pay the £10 initiation fee, Frederic wrote to his editor explaining how important membership in the Savage would be to writing his dispatches.[9] For at the club he could meet and know many contemporaries of stature in England—journalists, artists, actors, and dramatists—and from them he could get much of the news for the *Times.*

Besides, the Savage was just a few steps from his office at the Lancaster House, Savoy Place, on the Strand. He spent much of his time at the club writing and entertaining his friends. Arthur Warren, in his obituary, noted in fact that

Frederic passed "three-fourths of his time" at the Savage Club.[10] And Watson wrote that Frederic, whom he considered a "brilliant, high-spirited, hail-fellow-well-met sort of man . . . was soon one of the most popular members of the club."[11] For five years, at least, Frederic was more often at the Savage than at his office in the Strand. Thereafter, he made active his membership in the National Liberal Club, even though he continued to take occasional dinners at the Savage and to introduce American acquaintances to the members.[12]

Unquestionably, club life was for Frederic almost a necessity. The more than four hundred clubs that London's nearly five million inhabitants supported were the centers of much activity: social, political, artistic, and literary. Frederic almost at once perceived the value of club association; for as a foreign correspondent, he had to be close to the heart of the news; and in London in the 1880's and 1890's club gossip and acquaintances provided excellent copy, especially for a young newspaper man with Frederic's experience and insistent curiosity. Aaron Watson recounts a story that is indicative of Frederic's sharp awareness and of his readiness as a newsman. Watson walked out of the Savage one night to check the rumor of an attempt to blow up London Bridge. Frederic, scenting his friend's interest, followed Watson; got the story; and, when the reports were published, the two accounts were very much the same.[13]

One who reads Frederic's dispatches to the *Times* can, between the lines, envisage the young American listening to Sir Henry Irving tell of his plans for a new Shakespeare production at the Lyceum where, as actor-manager and associate of Miss Ellen Terry, he was drawing large crowds of theatergoers. Or perhaps one can imagine him as leaning over the bar with Arthur Wing Pinero and watching the dramatist as he sketched the details of a projected comedy. News flowed in the London clubs; and Frederic could not have missed much of it.

But what seems certain is that his articles on the cholera epidemic, his known association with eminent political figures in his own country, and his early club membership in London not only enhanced his value to the *Times* but also lent him prestige and position among his British contemporaries. At the very outset of his career in London he rose spectacularly into the front rank of journalists by making the best possible use of his associations for the work at hand. Yet it is possibly true, as his daughter wrote of him sixty-two years after his death, that "unhappily, success came too easily and too early to Harold Frederic."[14] "Unhappily," perhaps, because the life-pattern he was to weave in his last fourteen years became, for one who views it today, as intricate and complex as a map of London: the bold lines were interrupted here and there and broken or intersected by multiple and indistinct tangents.

II

There can be little doubt, for example, that even in his first year in England, lingering in his mind was the thought of writing a novel, a play, or a short story. Successful as he seems clearly to have been with his work for the *Times*, evidence points to dissatisfaction with the kind of life he was leading and to his desire to be free from it. On December 18, 1885, he wrote to Daniel Lamont, Private Secretary to President Cleveland:

> There are sundry phases of this *Times* connection which I am growing to dislike. I am very far from the idea of quitting, but the notion of getting into a more independent attitude financially, which would enable me to say what I would and what I would not do, grows upon me. I have therefore been thinking about asking for the new post of Consular Inspector for Great Britain, contemplated (as report goes) by the Administration.[15]

What Lamont replied has not yet been discovered, if it ever will be. Frederic had written him at the beginning of the same year (February 26) with typical self-confidence, but seriously:

> I have it in mind to write you a long letter soon, on the subject of the Consular service in Great Britain, the men here, their work as it is, and as it might be. I can't make you promise to read it after you get it, but at least you are going to get it. I want to harangue you, too, on the subject of a reorganization in the Consular branch of the State office, where much of the present waste and weakness can best be remedied.[16]

Frederic had some reason, apparently, for thinking that he might qualify for the position about which he queried Lamont. But appointment did not come nor, so far as the record goes, even a request for an application.

Still, if Frederic had not the itch to write creatively when he first went to England, he was soon inspired to try his hand at a novel. He spent (as he said in the Preface to the Uniform Edition of *In the Sixties*) much time with a journalist friend, T. P. O'Connor, who had received two hundred and fifty dollars from the *Weekly Echo* "for a serial story, based upon his own observations as a youngster in Ireland. . . . He seemed to make his book with extreme facility, never touching the weekly installment until the day for sending it to the printer's had arrived, and then walking up and down dictating the new chapters in a very loud voice, to drown the racket of his secretary's typewriter. This appeared to be a highly simple way of earning two hundred and fifty dollars. . . ."[17] So he went home to start a story of his own at once. He took his first chapter to the editor of the *Weekly Echo,* Aaron Watson; but Watson told him that, though his fiction might do for an American audience, it was clearly not for English readers. Nevertheless, Frederic persisted and completed the first of his novels, *Seth's Brother's Wife.*

Seth was published first in serial form in the United States, but the English edition was not put onto the London market until November 17, 1887, by Frederic's London publisher, Chatto and Windus. Although the preface ten years later described his impulse to write, the book does not by any means reveal his hopes for it nor the soaring dreams he had of becoming a successful author who would be independent of his newspaper work, if not free from it altogether. In seeking the government appointment he probably had in mind what Liverpool had meant to Hawthorne and Venice to William Dean Howells. But *Seth* gave him assurance and a vision of what might be. As he readied his manuscript for *Scribner's Magazine* in 1886, he wrote to his young friend on the *Observer* staff in Utica, John Howe:

> I think I see independence close before me now. Tomorrow I shall write the last two chapters of my novel. There will then be a week of revision, of rewriting here and there;

> by March 10 the whole thing will be ready to send across the Atlantic to my publishers. . . . I have the backing of some of the best judges in England for saying that the thing will come perilously close to being the strongest story any American has written. I believe in it with an enthusiasm I never dreamed that my own work could awaken in me. Barrymore and I are at work—tentatively as yet—making a play out of the thing. Both together will make me independent—but not a word about it yet.
>
> If these beliefs of mine are not bubbles, I shall come back to America in 1887 with some money, with a reputation, and with the manuscript of a second story—the Mohawk Valley romance [*In the Valley*] which I began five years ago—in such shape that two months' pointing up on the ground will make it in American literature what Henry Esmond is in English. Then I need never, please God, ask what time a paper goes to press again.[18]

Frederic's expectations for *Seth's Brother's Wife* were not, alas, realized; and his fervent wish for independence and freedom from his duties to the *Times* was never to become a reality. *Seth* found only a moderate-sized reading public in both England and the United States; and the play form aborted. How much of the play version Barrymore wrote or edited cannot now be determined for the manuscript is entirely in Frederic's hand. But if the play came to naught and if the novel did not sell so well as he had hoped it would, he yet remained confident. Steadfastly keeping at his manuscripts, he published in 1890 both *In the Valley,* which has been reprinted twice since it first was introduced to the reading public, and *The Lawton Girl* which, he said, "suggested itself at the outset as a kind of sequel to *Seth's Brother's Wife*."[20] Chatto and Windus paid him only £25 for the English rights to *Seth* and £75 a little over two years later for *The Lawton Girl*—hardly enough to encourage him to resign his position with the *Times*.[21] What royalties he received from Scribner's from the sale of these books cannot be discovered; but they did not, for the kind of life he chose to lead, suffice to make him independent of newspaper deadlines.[22]

III

Frederic's hope, too, that he might return to his "native heath" is reflected in his nostalgic words "I shall come back to America in 1887 with some money, with a reputation. . . ." Probably, when he wrote young Howe, the remembrance of home and of the simpler, more intimate kind of life he had enjoyed in Utica and Albany was still freshly with him. His early books dealing with his beloved Mohawk Valley kept the memory of those days vividly in the forefront of his thinking. Although the first eighteen months of London life had doubtless excited and challenged him, the excitement had worn off. It is apparent that when his bubbles burst he learned to accept, despite his impatience, altered hopes and to count only upon occasional trips to the homeland to satisfy his longing.[23]

Meantime, he had to adjust to an entirely different order of existence and to move with a quite different kind of people from those with whom he had been associated in upstate New York. London, long a world capital, was paradoxically cosmopolitan and distinctly British at the same time. Life there was a far remove from that of the small cities in which Frederic had grown to young manhood and in which the comfortable routine of home to office in the morning and back home again in the evening was an easy and acceptable pattern of life. Given the rare treat of a play at the local theater, a party at the Baxters, or a weekend devoted to fishing in the nearby streams, Frederic was happy. Now, as the sole *Times* correspondent in London, he had to be at his office to open and answer his mail; to make regular trips to the houses of Parliament where legislation affecting England and, in fact, the whole world, might on any day be framed and passed; to stop in his clubs—in the eighties, the Savage, in the nineties, the National Liberal—where he added to his store of news and wrote his dispatches. The tempo of his life increased, as did the diversity of friends and acquaintances.

As his life became more complex, Frederic's character altered and matured. It did not mellow. To the contrary, he became more insistently individualistic. But his friends regarded him as completely sincere and honest and always intolerant of sham. Arthur Warren, his journalist colleague and friend, described him as the "frankest man in two hemispheres," and portrayed him as the "high-voiced, careless, over-generous, pugnacious, gentle-hearted, hardworked, dogmatic Frederic of Fleet Street and the smoking room."[24] In this succinct character sketch Warren revealed the great intricacy of Frederic's nature with all its curious contradictions and compulsions. Another friend, Robert Barr, saw him as "a man of huge, commanding presence, fierce of aspect, with a gruff voice calculated to strike terror into those who did not know him" but as a man of gentleness and kindliness and honesty beneath this awesome surface.[25]

In effect, Frederic was a nineteenth-century Dr. Johnson, so far as his English friends were concerned. Clement Shorter, editor of London's *Sketch,* noted Frederic's roughness of manner but considered it as only superficial. Bluntness in Dr. Johnson had, after all, been regarded as independence; and Frederic was, above all else, extremely independent. He had a limitless self-confidence and self-assurance that made him seem somewhat aloof at times. Nevertheless, as Frank Harris noted, Frederic possessed great charm which he exercised particularly upon his intimate friends. Harris recognized Frederic's propensity for disregarding social conventions and admitted that his aggressiveness on occasion amounted almost to a kind of callousness; but, at the same time, he insisted that Frederic's magnetism was so great and his friendliness so spontaneous that offenses were quickly forgiven.[26]

Sometimes, like Dr. Johnson, Frederic was careless of his manners. On one occasion, having been asked to entertain the guests at a dinner party, he got up, his napkin "dangling from his waist—he was rather an untidy man—and sang a series of American college songs roisterously, boisterously, yet, when occasion demanded it, with feeling and emotion."[27] At a similar event he was at the piano singing folk songs, balancing, meanwhile, a "piece of bread-and-butter and a piece of cake" on one knee—the crumbs of each decorating his waistcoat. Yet, the college songs he appeared to know much better than most college boys know them. Like Dr. Johnson, he seemed to be acquainted with everything and everybody.[28]

Frederic loved the conviviality that he found at parties and at his clubs. Yet he loved good talk equally well. In an age when conversation counted much more than today, he was rated as a quite remarkable conversationalist. Clement Shorter maintained that many men would run into the clubs at night primarily to hear Frederic talk; and talk Frederic assuredly would, far into the night and on into the morning, never wearying his listeners.[29] At the Ghouls, a club whose membership included James M. Barrie, Conan Doyle, Joseph Pennell, W. E. Henley, and Bernard Partridge, the cartoonist for *Punch,* Frederic presided over both food and conversation. A new chairman was supposed to be elected at each meeting held at Signor Roma's restaurant in High Holborn, but Frederic as a rule took over the management of these affairs. On the afternoon of the evening on which the men assembled, he ordered the menu and then tyrannized over the membership in such a jovial manner that no one complained.[30]

Like Dr. Johnson, too, Frederic appeared to have an almost universal knowledge. His curiosity was immense and he was said to have an almost photographic memory for details. He knew British aristocracy, for example, not just out of *Burke's Peerage.* His information was, as Aaron Watson indicated, amazingly up to date; for Frederick knew the names and ranks, the relationships, and the marriages. To Watson, it seemed that "no citizen of the United States could have possessed a more incongruous accomplishment; but it no doubt greatly increased his value to the New York *Times.*"[31] Clement Shorter wrote that even if to an Englishman Frederic's dispatches were occasionally irritating, Frederic unquestionably revealed an immense fund of information. "I have seen . . . Frederic," Shorter maintained, "in a time of a General Election with a notebook crammed with figures, and with a grip on the whole political situation in England the like of which probably was possessed by not half a dozen men, apart from the official wire-pullers. His grasp of facts was . . . astonishing. . . ."[32]

However, not all the information that Frederic worked so indefatigably to gather was of value to the *Times* only. Much of it, as his notes in the Library of Congress collection disclose, he used in the books that he wrote. What he had gleaned from his study of *Burke's Peerage* and other sources concerned with the British or Irish aristocracy he aptly utilized in *The Return of the O'Mahony* and *Gloria Mundi.* What he wrote about his preparation for the creation of a novel clearly reveals not only his driving desire to extend the limits of his knowledge but also a diligence of uncommon proportions. He had *Theron Ware* in mind when he stated that he set himself to the task of knowing everything that his characters knew. Four of them in *Ware,* as he once said, "happened to be specialists in different professions. . . . For instance, one of them is a biologist, who, among other things, experiments on Lubbock's and Darwin's lines. Although these pursuits are merely mentioned," Frederic wrote, "I got up masses of stuff on bees and cross-fertilization of plants. . . ."[33] Actually, the demands he made upon himself in order to be acccurate were a part of his newspaper training, but the same impulse drove him in the writing of his fictions: not so much detail piled indiscriminately upon detail, but detail placed accurately, whether it had to do with the menu at a particular restaurant in *March Hares,* or the balcony in a hotel window in Montreux in *The Market-Place.*

One of Frederic's avocational interests was bookbinding, a hobby that had a practical as well as ornamental value. One of his sons states that behind Old House on Dunsany Road in Brook Green, Hammersmith (the last of the London homes in which Grace and her children lived), was a large, two-story brick structure that in the days of the Regency had probably served as a carriage house.[34] The room on the second floor of this building was fitted out as both library and workshop. It contained a fine, revolving bookcase; one wall was lined with filled bookshelves. Across the room were other shelves filled in part with bookbinding materials. And on a workbench to the rear of the room were presses and a glue pot heated by gas. Frederic had a vast collection of press clippings on "every conceivable subject of interest to him." These he bound, indexed meticulously, and placed on two large shelves for ready reference. To others, his procedure for the preparation of his research materials might seem odd; but his bookbinding gave him some relaxation at the same time that it served a useful purpose. When he and Grace had lived on Bedford Square, he was only three minutes from the British Museum; but when he moved his family first to Surbiton and thence to Hammersmith, he probably became more and more dependent upon his own library.

Frederic traveled a good deal during the first several years of his residence in England. His earliest adventure on the Continent has already been described; but before he had been two months in London, he went to Ireland and later returned there many times. In fact one of the last vacation jaunts he took before he died was to County Cork and to the O'Mahony country. While he was in the midst of writing his novel, *The Return of the O'Mahony,* he spent nearly two weeks there, fishing and refreshing himself on some of the details of his work. For the *Times* he made numerous trips to the Continent: to Berlin, to Paris, to Brussels, and to other large cities. In Germany he collected enough information to write a biographical study of William II, entitled *The Young Emperor,* which was generally fairly well received.

Frederic's appointment diary for 1891 reveals that he sent the manuscript of *The Young Emperor* to the printers on May 20. Between July 22 and August 19 of the same year, he traveled, however, through many cities in Russia to report to his newspaper on a Jewish pogrom then raging in that country. His dispatches were collected in the following year and published by Putnam's in New York and by Heinemann in London under the title, *The New Exodus.* But on his return trip he routed himself through Buda Pesth, Vienna, Munich, and Frankfurt; and again in 1892 he went to Germany, this time to Bremen, Hessenhausen, Hildesheim, Goslar, Harzburg, and Broeken. Yet despite his moving about, he found some time for his writing. He noted in his appointment diary for 1892 that (probably in Harzburg) he "worked on 'Snarl,'" a manuscript never completed.

Frederic managed to do an astounding number of things, and he did them well. But he would have frustrated Boswell. To follow, in sequence, his day's course would have been impossible then as now. Had he left appointment diaries for all the years he spent in London, his life could more readily be pieced together. As it is, only three journals—for the years 1891, 1892, and 1893—remain; and the last one is only sparsely filled. The first two, however, give us a fair sample of the restlessness of his activity. Here, for example, are a few entries for the year 1892 that mark some typical progress:

> May 20. Began Copperhead; July 22. Finished Copperhead begun May 20; July 26. Fishing at Dilkes [Sir Charles Dilkes had long been a friend.]; July 29. Letter to Cleveland; July 30. The Copperhead to Scribner's . . .

Another series of dates runs as follows:

> November 8. Cleveland elected; November 18. Ruby left school; November 19. *Eve of Fourth* to Century; *Philistia;* November 24. Thanksgiving at Pennells; December 5. Began *War Widow;* December 29. *War Widow to Ill. London News;* December 31. *War Widow* to *Independent;* February 6, 1893. Shorter accepted *War Widow.* 30 Gs. [Guineas]; February 15. Dine at Dilkes. N. Y. Times–Gladstone; February 17. Began *The Deserter.* House in evening [Parliament].[35]

Many entries were, of course, never made, and one must fill the gaps with such expected activities as home and office would demand, with lunches or dinners at clubs, with letters to write, and with names of people to meet and interview. But those recorded indicate that through the years Frederic managed somehow and with some regularity to work on his fiction, no matter how pressed he might be with his duties for the *Times.* Such notations as that of *Philistia,* for example, on November 19, leave little to be imagined. Frederic began a series of satirical articles—"Observations in Philistia"—for the *National Observer* on February 20, 1892, and completed it on December 23, 1893. All but two of these articles were collected and finally published in 1896 by John Lane, at the Bodley Head, London, and by Merriam in New York, under the title of *Mrs. Albert Grundy.* Though Frederic affected a kind of light romance in the entire series, the whole is a plotless commentary upon bourgeois London society rather than a well-constructed narrative.

This book testifies, however, to Frederic's great range of interest and achievement. It also indicates not only his growth in stature as a writer but the acceptance he met in London generally. For *Mrs. Albert Grundy* was one of a set of six volumes that John Lane called the "Mayfair Set," other volumes being written by G. S. Street, Gerald Campbell, H. G. Wells, George Fleming, and Elizabeth Robins. Furthermore, in contributing to the *National Observer,* Frederic joined such distinguished company as Mallarmé, Kipling, Stevenson, Yeats, Alice Meynell, Pennell, and J. M. Barrie. So it was to go from the moment he penned in his firm, even, beautifully legible handwriting the opening lines of *Seth's Brother's Wife.*

IV

How Grace Williams Frederic responded to her hearty, bluff, over-generous, extravagant husband and to a life altered by the rush—at times the almost frenzied activity—in which he was involved is not a happy story to tell. That she loved him through their early years goes without question. But London frightened and shocked her. She was essentially a Utica girl, happier by far in the uncomplicated domestic arrangement of her upstate New York homes, and so she remained. Reared by conventional Welsh and English parents, she was quite unsuited to the sophisticated society in which her husband expected her to move. Occasionally of course she gave dinners; she also gave teas, but she never *went* to any. She sought to be a good mother to her children; but, as the years passed, she drew more and more away from active participation in her husband's affairs. Toward the last of her life she was almost a recluse and her eldest daughter, Ruth, was her only companion.[36]

While they were still living at 12 Pembridge Crescent, off Bayswater in the Kensington District, Grace bore Harold his first son—another Harold—on July 10, 1885, hardly a year after their arrival in England. She lost this boy two years later, just as she had lost a little daughter in New York. Possibly because of the addition to his family and possibly, too, because he had never had a firm commitment from the *Times* about his expense account, Frederic complained bitterly to Charles R. Miller, his chief. But as he turned in his expenses, he found himself in some difficulties with the *Times* management over his seeming extravagances; and with Mr. Miller's reply came some wise counsel about economy and heedful attention to the way he managed his finances.[37] In order to effect a savings, therefore, and to keep his relations with the home office harmonious, Frederic moved his growing family some time after December 1, 1885, to less costly quarters at 8 Osnaburgh Terrace, by Regent's Park in northwest London.[38]

But Frederic was not a man to watch the pennies. Added income from books and stories encouraged him to move his family in 1887 to 39 Bedford Square and in this substantial mansion close to the British Museum he lived until 1892. There Grace bore a second and a third son, Hereward, on January 27, 1887, and another Harold on September 15, 1889, the latter taking the place of the first Harold who had died. From Bedford Square Frederic could walk quickly to his office on the Strand: to Oxford and down Charing Cross Road, passing the booksellers' shops on his way to Trafalgar Square and thence to Whitehall Place and the National Liberal Club, or back to the Strand and on to the Savage. High Holborn, Signor Roma's restaurant, and the meetings of the Ghouls were a convenient five minutes from his new home. The Museum, where he spent many hours "getting up" material for his articles for the *Pall Mall Gazette* and *Budget* or for his dispatches, was scarcely far enough away to allow him to finish the cigar that he had lit at home and puffed while he scanned the morning paper. One can see him as he chewed both cigar and moustache and muttered imprecations over a disturbing item in the daily news. "God's trousers," he would say.

Grace did not accompany her husband on his trips to the Continent or to Ireland and rarely was his consort at dinners or theater parties in the city. Ruth, his eldest child, served as his companion. Occasionally Frederic would take his daughter on walking trips into the country. They would go by train to some village in the countryside—almost anywhere—and then walk for a day or two, stopping for meals and over night at some inn. But this relationship was one of friends, not of father and daughter; for Frederic had almost nothing of the paternal instinct in him. Occasionally, too, Frederic would take his lovely young daughter on short trips to the Continent, much as Joel Thorpe took his niece and nephew for the Grand Tour in *The Market-Place*. And in London, he would escort her to a dinner (she would meet him at the National

Liberal Club) and the theater afterward, where he went for the first night performances that he reviewed in his dispatches to the *Times*. Or when he could not himself attend a play, Ruth would pile her hair on top of her head, slip into an evening gown, watch the performance, and the next day report her views on the play to her father. Relying on her judgment, Frederic would go to his study and prepare his notes for the press.

No matter where he lived, Frederic would have his study; and he insisted that his whims be catered to. He liked his pipes and his favorite Arcadia Mixture. In the "Old House" study at Brook Green, a room lined on three sides by bookshelves twelve feet high, he made an orderly arrangement, next to his desk, of tobacco, a first-edition set of Johnson's dictionary, a bottle of Appollinaris mineral water, and Montaigne's *Essays*. Wherever he could, he had a garden, but he was not often in it; and for his greenhouse, usually attended by his daughter, Ruth, he bought rare plants. But he loved growing things and knew the names and species of the plants he purchased, an interest and knowledge reflected in *Theron Ware*, *Gloria Mundi*, and *The Market-Place*. Whether at Bedford Square, at Surbiton, or at Brook Green, Frederic wrote, Grace occasionally entertained their friends, and the children had their nurses and their schooling. The outward aspect of domestic felicity was everywhere present.

Yet clearly not all was as it should have been between Harold and Grace Frederic. At some time, probably early in 1890, Frederic met and fell in love with Miss Kate Lyon. *March Hares* is believed to contain some elements of the truth about their meeting, but it seems quite possible that they found one another in the British Museum.

Kate Lyon was born in Oswego, New York, in 1853. Moving to Chicago, she graduated from the Cook County Normal School in 1870 and taught in one of the early grammar schools. When her sister and brother-in-law, Mary (May) Lyon and Frank Richie went to England, she went with them, helping May with the care of her four little children. Kate's mother's maiden name was O'Mahony, probably of the County Cork O'Mahonys; and it is almost certain that Frederic's interest in the O'Mahony name and the fine comedy that he built around it were inspired by this relationship. He named the heroine of his Irish novel, *The Return of the O'Mahony,* after Kate Lyon.[39]

Frederic would have nothing to do with a clandestine relationship. How he prevailed upon Kate to live with him openly as his wife cannot easily be explained; but he did and she bore him three children: Helen, born in 1892; Heloise, in 1893; and Barry, in 1894. Frederic rented for Kate a fine big house called "Homefield" about fifteen miles south of London and beautifully situated in Caterham Valley on a part of the Surrey Downs in Kenley—today a part of a large suburban development but then only a hamlet. He divided his time between his two households; as a rule he devoted the weekends to Grace and her children and the rest of the time, or at least the part of it when he was not at work in the city, to Kate.

All evidence points to a happy union between Harold Frederic and Kate Lyon. In the eight or nine years that they lived together in this fashion, they entertained many of Frederic's friends and among them, toward the last, were Stephen and Cora Crane. The Cranes' first home in England—Ravensbrook, in Oxted, Surrey—Kate and Frederic often visited; and they took the Cranes with them on vacation trips to Ireland. After Frederic's death, Kate helped Stephen with the research for his *Great Battles of the World;* in fact, extant letters reveal that she must have done much of the basic writing for that book. They indicate, too, that she wrote with great charm and vivacity, reflecting the kind of personality that had so strong an attraction for Harold Frederic.[40]

Nevertheless, just how Frederic managed to preserve the social amenities in both homes is hard to imagine. If Kate was happy, it must be said that Grace was cruelly unhappy and withdrew more than ever into herself. Frederic did not count the cost either to Grace and her children or to Kate and hers; nor, apparently, did he give much thought to the tragic circumstances into which he might—and by his early death, did—plunge them all. Whether he ever regretted his extravagant bargain he did not disclose.

Although the support of two families would not have been a burden for a wealthy man, Frederic had only limited means and was forced by necessity to earn more and more money as the list of his dependents grew. No record of his having been given a raise in salary by the *Times* management can be found. He could turn only to his writing of fiction and non-fiction for the needed increment, and the volume of his publications after 1890 is weighty evidence that he felt the pressure to produce. Had he been a better manager of financial affairs the strain might have been less severe, but it would be unfair to call him merely improvident. His last accounts, drawn up by his lawyers and reposing now in the Frederic Collection in the Library of Congress, show that he died rather heavily in debt. More significantly, his letters divulge the embarrassment he must have suffered from his need to juggle his financial arrangements and to ask again and again for advances on royalties. From time to time he turned impatiently upon publishers who were slow to pay him his due.

On February 7, 1894, as the following letters indicate, he was already feeling the pinch. He wrote one of the McClures in America:

> I wrote to your brother about the Gladstone article, and the payment for it, some time ago, but have had no answer. . . . You say the pay will be forthcoming in "about a month." I should be glad, if, when you return the article, you could make an exact date within the month on which I can count. I practically discounted the thing with my bankers in my 1893 accounts, as a man who works for a living is obliged to do, and I can't afford to have it go along indefinitely into 1894.

Then on March 14, of the same year, he wrote again:

> What is the good of telling me what you want done with the Gladstone thing, and the boy's story, and how soon you want it, when you don't send me the MSS? And furthermore, I am not at all disposed to do further work on these things, and to accept the very little pay which you offer for them, *unless* there is a distinct and satisfactory date fixed for that payment.
>
> I am kept in a perpetual worry and annoyance by the slipshop money-methods of two-thirds of the American publishers I have relations with—and I am resolute about not

widening the area of this unhappiness. . . . I did the Gladstone thing in time rather cheekily stolen from other work, simply to help you out. But if I am to do more on it—and I could get £100 elsewhere for the comprehensive article you now suggest—there must be no fooling about the money down.[41]

Even as late as December 31, 1897, Frederic wrote to Charles Willoughby Dayton, an eminent New York lawyer who represented certain of Frederic's book interests in this country, asking that royalties be deposited to his account in the Lincoln bank. In the same letter he said he had heard it rumored that some American playwrights were attempting to pirate a dramatization of one of his novels; and he suggested that Dayton look into the matter to make sure that proper payment for publishing rights would be secured. On July 15, 1898, he sent another letter to Dayton, expressing fear that the Chicago publisher, Stone, who was said to be squandering his money in England, might not meet his financial obligations to his authors. Frederic had some reason to be fearful about Mr. Stone; for Stone and Kimball, who had published his *Damnation of Theron Ware,* went bankrupt and Frederic lost from the sale of his book in the United States. Now Stone, who had re-established his company, was to publish *Gloria Mundi* after its serialization in the *Cosmopolitan.*[42]

A letter dated October 5 (no year given) from William Heinemann, Frederic's London publisher of the later fiction and non-fiction, further shows Frederic's plight:

My dear Frederic,
Your request for £30 puts me into a fix. My partner finds that you have had nearly £50 more than your books have earned in loans and unfortunately the books are bringing in very little.

Another from Sydney S. Pawling, Heinemann's partner, makes further disclosures:

At Heinemann's request I have gone into your a/c with great care and find that if we increase the Royalty on "New Exodus" to 25% it is absolutely the limit to which we can

> go. . . . I may add that so far as I know 25% is the highest royalty ever paid in England.

In still another, somewhat pitiable note, addressed to "My dear Jack" (probably John Scott Stokes who was to become his executor) Frederic wrote:

> Here is all I raised at the S. [aturday] R. [eview] yesterday. They owe me some £30 or £35 more, but the accounts beyond December aren't made up yet.
>
> Other things are coming in in a few days, and I shan't keep you waiting a day longer than necessary.[43]

Frederic was never to be free from financial worries. When he died his advances on royalties from Heinemann were still far in excess of what his books had brought in.

To say, however, that he wrote potboilers in order to clear up his deficits would be decidedly unjust. No one knew better than he the lonely business of writing: the searching of the storehouse of the mind and the toil of making the words flow onto the blank sheet of paper—and with his conscience ready to rebuke him for wrong words used. When G. B. Burgin, one of his English friends, once remarked to Frederic that a man should not be judged by his life but by his work, Frederic, sensitive to what others might think of his domestic divigations, cut him off quickly, saying: "Enough of that. Whatever my life has been, my pen has always been on the side of the angels."[44] And perhaps no one ever made a fairer estimate of Frederic than he did of himself. Those who knew him best have testified to his integrity and to his thorough honesty.

But even for a man who seemed to have no limit to the physical energy he could spend, the pace which Frederic set for himself was at last too rapid. In mid-August of 1898, he suffered a stroke, probably an embolism in the brain. Impatient with illness, and more impatient still with doctors or with healers of any kind, Frederic refused to follow orders, to rest, or to diet. "Doctor," he said to one physician called in to attend him, "I have an intellectual contempt for milk."[45] He *would* have his cigars and pipe, his brandy, his rides in the country. For two months he struggled manfully against death, refusing to believe that he could die, or to face the reality of his condition. As his daughter later wrote: "It probably never dawned upon him until he lay dying, that at last he was face to face with something that was stronger than he."[46]

Though his family and friends recognized the gravity of his illness, his death on October 19, 1898, at Homefield, came to them as a shock. Kate was with him; so was his young daughter, Ruth. He had lived only two months beyond his forty-second birthday.

CHAPTER 4

Before the Damnation

I *Seth's Brother's Wife*

THE READER who expects to find a steady, consistent line of development in Harold Frederic's fiction is bound to be puzzled at first by what he finds in *Seth's Brother's Wife*. In all the stories he had written before 1885 Frederic left seemingly clear indication that when at last he came to write a sustained work, it would be historical, romantic, derivative, and sentimental. But *Seth's Brother's Wife* is none of these. It is instead a powerfully realistic study of contemporary life in America, completely free from its author's perennial dependence upon Erckmann-Chatrian, and with little of the sentimentality and melodrama that mar his early short tales, both published and unpublished. *Seth's Brother's Wife* flatly defies explanation in view of Frederic's first exercises in fiction, for this first novel reflects life and hard-bitten experience in the real world of the 1870's and 1880's, and not the dim and history-bound one which existed only in the minds of two French story-tellers.

The writing of *Seth* also represented an abrupt change in Frederic's old, but vague, plans for his own career as an author. For ten unproductive years—since the days when Horatio Seymour's Oriskany Centennial speech had set his mind to bubbling—he had been planning a novel about the Mohawk Valley during the Revolution. Nothing had come of these plans except an accumulation of historical documentation that bewildered him when he considered putting it to fictional account. By 1885, as has been noted, he still "did not know how to make a book of any kind, let alone an historical book of the kind which should be the most difficult and exacting of all."[1] And so, with a nothing-to-lose air, he started to write "a contemporary story" with a double purpose in mind: to try for some comparatively easy money, and also to learn how "to make a book." *Seth's Brother's Wife,* then, was conceived as a trial novel, deliberately but rather casually begun as an exercise to prepare him for what he considered to be more important work.

Ten energetic months later, on February 27, 1886, Frederic wrote to his Utica friend, John B. Howe, the letter in which he expressed his confident hopes for success and independence (see pp. 57-58).[2] In another six weeks, the book was an accomplished fact, well on its way toward publication. "I have written a novel," wrote Frederic to Daniel Lamont, Cleveland's secretary, on April 24, "and I have today cabled to Scribner's my acceptance of their proposals for its publication—which are exceedingly liberal. The book will probably be out in June."[3]

He was wrong about the publication date, for the publishers had planned to introduce the novel as a serial in the new *Scribner's Magazine,* beginning with its first number in January, 1887. Not until some months later, when Frederic's name and work were already familiar to the thousands of readers who enthusiastically received the new magazine, did the work appear in book form.[4]

It was natural that this first novel should be told against the thunder of the political and editorial warfare that Frederic had so recently witnessed in upstate New York. And since his was a bold, analytical mind, well equipped by both nature and training to move from the abstract manifestations of political theory to the concrete machinery of day-to-day organizational tactics, it was also natural that he should discuss these abstractions in concrete terms, against the landscape and among the people of an area with which he was intimately familiar: upstate New York in the guiltiest days of the Gilded Age.

At its simplest level, *Seth's Brother's Wife* tells of the rise of one Fairchild, Seth, and the fall of another, Albert. In two closely integrated plots in which both brothers play major roles (a third brother, John Fairchild, is a secondary character), Frederic explores the condition of two kinds of morality, public and private, in an area of upstate New York much like the one that had produced him. The Fairchild brothers are part of an old New York family whose once-bright star has been in eclipse for two ineffectual generations. The novel opens as their mother lies dead in the run-down Fairchild farmhouse and their father seems ready to die. Albert, the oldest of the brothers, returns to the family home as a wealthy and successful New York lawyer who cares nothing for the farm except as a legal residence from which to embark on the brilliant political career he is planning for himself. Seth, the youngest brother, is sent off to the small city of Tecumseh, where Albert has arranged a job for him with a daily newspaper much like the Utica *Observer* whose operations Frederic knew so well.

As the "private" plot unfolds, Seth Fairchild grows into a responsible editorial position after making and paying for numerous minor mistakes along the way. Just as Harold Frederic's rise had been rapid on the *Observer,* so is Seth's on the Tecumseh *Chronicle.* When an initially harmless epistolary flirtation with Isabel—Albert Fairchild's bored, attractive, and childless young wife—leads him to the edge of a serious affair with his own sister-in-law, Seth is saved from ugly moral consequences by providential chance rather than by his own strength of will.

Meanwhile the second, or "public," plot has been developing. Albert Fairchild's dream of going to Congress, originally a simple ambition, has turned into a sinister plot to buy a nomination. He succeeds in subverting a few key political and editorial figures but antagonizes others. Both the owner of Seth's paper and finally Seth himself refuse to support Albert; they declare instead for Richard Ansdell, a dynamic idealist-reformer with a strong talent for practical politics. Albert also fails to touch Abe Beekman, the local political boss. Beekman, honest himself, despises rich, arrogant political amateurs who mistakenly assume that all local leaders wear price tags. In a frantic last-minute attempt to reach and buy the convention that is about to reject him and nominate Ansdell, Albert Fairchild is waylaid and murdered for the intended bribe money by his own lieutenant, Milton Squires. As the novel ends, the murderer has been caught and punished,

Ansdell has been elected as the standard-bearer of honest and forward-looking government, and Seth's career shows continuing promise. In a final gratuitous touch that surprises not only the reader but the other characters as well, Seth's brother's wife, the erstwhile temptress and now Albert's widow, captures and marries the new congressman, Ansdell.

So much for a brief summary of a complicated story. Clearly, however, *Seth's Brother's Wife* is worthy of critical examination that goes beyond its two intertwined plots. Behind both are a background and an array of minor characters so richly and at times so grimly delineated that they sometimes distract the reader from the real point of the novel. For instance, Vernon Louis Parrington—one of the most formidable commentators of another generation—was so distracted that he read *Seth's Brother's Wife* as "a drab tale of farm life in upper York State, as bitter as any tale of the western border. It is a story of defeat," Parrington went on, "of flight from country to town. . . . The slack servants, gossipy and impudent, the petty lives, the grasping ways unrelieved by any grace or beauty, and set in a world of petty machine politics, make a drab and unattractive picture. Harold Frederic evidently hates this countryside that bred him."[5]

This Procrustean observation, which trims *Seth's Brother's Wife* to fit Parrington's own brilliantly conceived thesis, actually mistakes the nonessentials for the novel itself. Bemused by the brilliance of Frederic's touches of local color, Parrington saw only the bleak setting and missed the drama proper, which is fundamentally comic in both plan and execution. Frederic, as the reader knows, had not been bred in the "countryside," and so the novel is no simple chronicle of the author's own "flight from country to town." Furthermore, Frederic would have been startled to hear that he "hated" the countryside that he described. Even as he wrote the final chapters of *Seth,* he was in fact happily planning a long vacation trip back to it.[6] Nor is there any real "defeat" in *Seth's Brother's Wife* except for the carefully intended one of lax morality: of Isabel's plans for dalliance with her naïve young brother-in-law, and Albert's plans for a career built on chicanery and corruption. In this novel Frederic had a more positive purpose in mind than Parrington and other critics were able to see behind the portrayal of "slack servants" and a "drab and unattractive" farmyard.

In the letter to Lamont already quoted, Frederic himself provided the key that makes *Seth's Brother's Wife* something quite different from the angry and bitter tract that Parrington saw in it. "The story is laid in rural Central New York," Frederic wrote Lamont, "and deals with farm-life, politics, and newspaper work in a provincial city. The action lies in the campaign of 1882 (which perhaps you will remember. If you don't the Governor will). It is full of character, political and social. . . . The whole thing is between the good and bad in politics."[7]

And so the real purpose, which is clear enough in the story itself but becomes increasingly obvious when *Seth's Brother's Wife* is read in the context of Frederic's other American fiction, is to show the gradual resurgence of the political integrity (synonymous to Frederic with public morality) of a community which has too long tolerated the arrogant machinations of corrupt and complacent public leaders—the "bad" in politics. He dramatizes this resurgence in his development of three characters representative of the regional population at three different organizational levels: Seth Fairchild, who survives attacks on his integrity not only as an individual but also as a member of a "county family" and as a newspaperman with a moral obligation to his area; Abe Beekman, the incorruptible local "boss," the career politician who knows how to move the people to positive action; and Richard Ansdell, the inspiring "practical idealist" who—with the assistance of individuals like Seth and organizations like Beekman's—brings about the political (i.e., moral) regeneration of the community that had too long shown only apathy toward the need for integrity and morality in high public places.

In his first novel, Frederic was not concerned with political programs like the Populist agrarianism that Parrington looked for; unlike Hamlin Garland, Frederic was interested in *men*—in political leaders, rather than in political programs. The real social purpose of *Seth's Brother's Wife* was to demonstrate, in a tone of restrained optimism, that in spite of a certain drabness and apparent moral and spiritual laxity of life in upstate New York, the region could still produce from its own citizenry honest and devoted leaders who were capable of arousing the moral vigor of the public when such vigor was needed: men like Ansdell, whose zeal "often swayed despite themselves the politicians of his party who had least in common with him and disliked him . . . even when they were being swept along toward nobler purposes than their own small souls could ever have conceived, in the current of feeling which his devotion had created."

Frederic himself had seen and known the "good" in politics in such leaders as Samuel J. Tilden, Horatio Seymour, and Grover Cleveland, to name only the most famous. At the lower echelons of political leadership he had seen honesty and integrity as well as the corruption usually ascribed almost automatically to the career political party man. There were any number of Abe Beekmans throughout the state—honest local leaders who worked at their jobs, who could get things done, and without whose knowledge of practical politics no reformer, however inspired, could ever hope to reach a position where his intentions could be achieved. And finally, Frederic himself had been a young Seth Fairchild: naïve, even ignorant of the ways of the political world, but thoroughly imbued with an ideal that strong and unscrupulous forces could not shake. Altogether, the stubborn but successful struggle of such men to save the body politic from its own apathetic self as well as from venal leaders seemed to Frederic to be eminently deserving of dramatic fictional treatment. *Seth's Brother's Wife* was to be a comedy, then; occasionally dark and bitter, to be sure, but nevertheless a comedy.

Only about two months before Frederic started to write *Seth's Brother's Wife,* his friend Grover Cleveland had been inaugurated as President of the United States. Shortly after the election, Frederic had written to Cleveland a highly rhetorical account of his recent fears for America:

> I do not know whether you feel as fully as I do that the public tendency since the war, in business, in politics, in social life, has rotted and infected almost every condition of our existence. Moral sensibility has been blunted, the keen edge of

> honor turned, the standards of justice clogged, the ardor of patriotism chilled, the confiding ignorance of the half-educated tampered with, the ambitions of good men perverted—until there is in these latter days a condition of things as gross and wretched in its way as that under which Germany, and in fact, all Continental Europe, weltered four hundred years ago.[8]

Cleveland's election to the Presidency, however, had bolstered his flagging faith, and his fears were lessened: ". . . the pride of country, of race, yes, of state, comes to me now. . . . It is true . . . that all the greed and scoundrelism and prejudice and folly of our political, race, and business sides, massed into one grand desperate effort for control, are not able to stand before the simple weight of an honest man and an upright cause."

In this mood of renewed but cautious optimism about his country's future, Frederic started to write his first novel in which the integrity and the moral fiber of an American community win out over "the greed and scoundrelism and prejudice and folly" of an age as he had seen it in concrete forms—especially in political conventions and campaigns—during his journalistic excursions up and down the Mohawk Valley. And fittingly enough, the action of *Seth's Brother's Wife* revolves around a political struggle very similar to the gubernatorial campaign in New York in 1882 in which Frederic himself had played a part and which had resulted in the election of Cleveland as governor.

Just as the "heroes" of *Seth's Brother's Wife*—Ansdell, Beekman, and Seth himself—are themselves products of the society which they lead in the assault on political corruption, so are the important "villains"—Albert Fairchild and his wife, Isabel—strangers who mistake simplicity and complacence for moral petrifaction. Albert, it is true, is Seth's brother, and a native of the region; but he has been away from it for so long that he has forgotten its ways. Isabel, of course, never knew them. Significantly, it is from the viewpoint of these two unsympathetic and condescending outsiders that most of the drabness and apparent emptiness of upstate rural life is described: Isabel, for example, sees that life in its worst light before she has even come to live on the farm. It is she who makes the long speech that is usually quoted out of context by critics anxious to show how Frederic "hated" his countryside:

> "Oh, it must be such a dreary life! . . . The dreadful people you have to know: men without an idea beyond crops and calves and the cheese-factory; women slaving their lives out doing bad cooking, scarce opportunities for intercourse with other women to the weakest and most wretched gossip; coarse servants who eat at the table with their employers and call them by their Christian names. . . ."

Thus Isabel Fairchild, just arrived from the city, indicts a rural society which she has not even seen. Seth's hesitant protest—"Oh, it isn't all so bad as you paint it, perhaps, Isabel. . . . You don't quite see it at its best here. . . ."—is ineffective on Isabel, who is wrongly convinced that the crudities she catalogues here are the significant characteristics of the life that lies around her.

Seth and Harold Frederic knew that there were other, more admirable characteristics. If anything, Isabel's dismal picture constitutes evidence of Frederic's integrity as a realist and his concern with the "elementary truth-telling" that Alfred Kazin has ascribed to Frederic's work in general. As Paul Haines has pointed out, Frederic was writing this passage not only soon after a tour of the cholera-stricken areas of southern France and Italy but when he was familiar with the sufferings of the Irish peasantry. He could hardly "have developed a sudden vision of the New York countryman as a victim of economic injustice. . . . Nor had he a sudden impulse to vilify the life either of the Mohawk countryside or of the town in which he had so propitiously begun his career. The farmers [of New York], however benighted, were no more bigoted than the middle-class Londoners who, as Frederic wrote, were organizing their despotism anew."[9] Isabel's chilling version of life on a New York State farm, in other words, is not the reflection of Frederic's own vision.

It is true, of course, that Isabel never does see this life "at its best," and neither does the reader. Pejorative description such as Isabel's suits Frederic's purpose in the novel; any form of idealization, on the other hand, would have destroyed the careful consistency with which Frederic tells the story of the growth of morality, both public and private, from what looks to be morally barren ground. In his other novels, Frederic was to allow himself intrusive comments which reveal his appreciation of the New York landscape and the sturdy, middle-class qualities that were his own birthright; he found no place for such comments, however, in *Seth's Brother's Wife*. Thus, he had a purposeful bleakness in his unflattering picture of the gossiping servants (who, with Beekman, speak with a dialect not imposed on the major characters); in his description of the rural funeral and burying-ground, with its crumbling memorials to yesterday's minor tyros; in his searing commentary on the bad taste of which rural undertakers are capable; on his remarks on the unique brutality of the "rural murderer," some of whose handiwork Frederic had actually seen during his days with the *Observer*.

And so, as the story moves toward a climax that is carefully foreshadowed even as the atmosphere seems grimmest, Frederic has pictured unpleasant facets of a kind of social life which seems, as he had written to Cleveland, to "have rotted and infected almost every condition" of upstate existence. But even as he describes these forbidding surfaces of his society Frederic is also uncovering the potentially powerful sense of public morality which can be seen dimly stirring first in the mild protests of John Fairchild (the third of the three brothers); then gaining momentum in the vigorous editorial stand taken by Mr. Workman, publisher of the newspaper which Seth edits; and finally culminating in the realistic person of Abe Beekman who is admirable in his scorn for those who, like Albert Fairchild, think that position is "all money." Finally, the triumph of Ansdell is not the triumph of a political innocent of the F. Marion Crawford variety, the amateur reformer who lives only in books, "drinking tea in some lady's drawing-room, declaiming to the fair sex on how he is going to reform politics." It is the triumph of a people whose long-forgotten sense of political responsibility has been aroused by able individuals prompted not so much by "programs" as by the simple purpose of restoring honesty and integrity to the public domain. Frederic's first novel is his affirmation of belief in the soundness of the political foundations and the underlying public morality of his own society. The affirmation is the more forceful because of his pejorative treatment of the unattractive social characteristics that as a realist, temporarily at least, he felt bound to report.

II *In the Valley*

Before the manuscript of his first novel was fairly out of his hands and on its way toward publication in *Scribner's Magazine,* Frederic was briskly at work on his second, ultimately published as *In the Valley*—"the real work," as he called it, "the book I had been dreaming of so long."[1] Brimming with a confidence that had come to him steadily as he wrote *Seth's Brother's Wife,* Frederic was at last able to articulate this story that had been haunting him for almost nine years, ever since the days of his involvement with the Oriskany Centennial Celebration of 1877. Several times during these years he had gone so far as to write out long sections (one of more than twenty thousand words), "but they were all failures."[2] As early as 1883, during his Albany editorship, the story had been clear in his mind, although it stubbornly refused to be written. One of his companions of that year recalls that as he and Frederic whiled away a rainy afternon during a fishing trip in the Mohawk country, Frederic told him the whole story of *In the Valley,* admitting that Horatio Seymour had provided the inspiration for the tale.[3] But two years later, in another country, he had nothing to show for his efforts but "an immense amount of material in the shape of notes, cross-references, dates, maps, biographical facts, and the like"[4] that he had carried across an ocean, hoping that some day, when he had learned how "to make a book," the material would be of use to him.

With the writing of *Seth,* he had finally learned how a book should be put together and he began the new work with a bold, confident hand. He wrote John Howe that he thought his Mohawk Valley romance would be to American literature what *Henry Esmond* had come to be to English literature (see pp. 57-58). By October, 1886, the novel was going so well that he could write Edward L. Burlingame, editor of Scribner's,

"You will know how to discount my statement of faith that it is to be the best thing of the kind ever done by an American."[5] Three months later, in January, 1887, half the novel was in Burlingame's hands over a title that brought shudders to the entire Scribner's staff: *Douw Mauverensen.* When the book was at last completed, it was Burlingame himself who supplied the title, after rejecting not only Frederic's first suggestion but his second, *Where the Mohawk Gently Glides.* Titled *In the Valley,* the romance ran as a serial in *Scribner's Magazine* before appearing in book form in 1890.[6]

In the Valley, Frederic's only full-length historical romance, is told against the background of the American Revolution as it was fought in upstate New York. Narrated in retrospect by its central character, Douw Mauverensen, the story proper opens in 1757 with an account of Douw's own boyhood days. After the death of his father, a Dutch Reformed minister, Douw's impoverished mother allows the boy to be taken into the home of "Mr. Stewart," a kind but mysterious Englishman with a bar sinister background and aristocratic sympathies which never rub off on Douw despite his lasting regard for his benefactor. Also a part of this "family" is an orphaned Palatine German waif named Daisy (short for Desideria), who grows up as Douw's sister in Mr. Stewart's pleasant Mohawk Valley home in the years before the Revolution when Sir William Johnson ruled the valley.

With Sir William's death the placid pattern of existence along the Mohawk is broken; the society that was contentedly united under the wise leadership of the benevolent baronet becomes divided under the oppressive arrogance of his heirs and their retainers—one of whom is Philip Cross, Douw's natural antagonist since childhood. Douw's loyalties in the class war that takes shape in the mid-1770's are with his own humble democratic neighbors who see their old liberties now threatened by a class of native would-be aristocrats, the Tories.

When Daisy, whom Douw has come to love as more than an adopted sister, marries Philip Cross, Douw sulks off to Albany in anger and disgust. He finally becomes part of the forces that General Nicholas Herkimer leads to meet St. Leger's army of British regulars and banished Tories who have threatened to despoil the valley. In the climactic event of the story, the Battle of Oriskany, Philip Cross—now one of the most dangerous of the Tories—is badly wounded, but is saved from death by Douw, whose capacity for hatred has now diminished. Philip is finally disposed of, however, in a manner which Douw cannot control. Douw marries the widowed Daisy, and all is contented reminiscence as the book ends.

Such is the plot of the long-planned work that Frederic intended as a response to the appeal he had heard Horatio Seymour make at the Oriskany Centennial for "records of the past" that "can become a part of the general intelligence of our people." Seymour's approval of the book, Frederic wrote in a dedicatory note dated 1890, more than four years after Seymour's death, "would have been the highest honor it could possibly have won." And almost certainly had he lived to read *In the Valley*, Seymour would have approved of the spirit in which the book was written, of the perception and feeling for New York history that shine through the occasionally contrived plot and wooden characters. For *In the Valley*, though not memorable for its banal love story, is important for the manner in which it traces the evolution of two groups of bitter and implacable enemies, the patriots and the Tories, within the mixed society that existed in the Mohawk Valley in the years leading up to the Revolution.

The novel is actually a dramatic treatment of Frederic's conviction that the Revolution in New York was really a civil war, with its own local dimensions: not a war of rebels against king, but of class against class. The population of the valley is a mixture of Germans, Dutch, Irish, Scotch, and English. "One cannot understand the terrible trouble which came upon us later," says Douw Mauverensen, the narrator, "without some knowledge of these race divisions." For a whole generation, the valley remains peaceful, safe, and outwardly content under the firm but benevolent despotism of Sir William Johnson, who uses his "fondness and faculty for attracting retainers and domineering subordinates to public advantage." While Sir William lives, the valley is safe from the outbreak of class antagonisms, which the "honest old baronet" effectively prevents by his mere presence.

As Sir William grows older, however, the arrogant behavior

and aristocratic pretensions of his son, Sir John Johnson, and his class-minded allies, the Butlers, foreshadow the end of peace and freedom in the valley. Even before Sir William dies it is plain that his heirs and their followers plan to impose a kind of feudal order on a society that has learned to love liberty. Actually, Douw realizes as he looks back,

> for years the gulf had been insensibly widening here under our noses, between the workers and idlers. . . . Something of this was true all over the Colonies: no doubt what I noticed was but a phase of the general movement. . . . But here in the valley, more than elsewhere, this broadening fissure of division ran through farms, through houses, ay, even through the groups gathered in front of the family fire-place—separating servants from employers, sons from fathers, husbands from wives.

No sooner is Sir William Johnson dead than the long-smoldering threat of class conflict flames up, and the valley populace quickly takes sides: the Tory aristocrats and their servile retainers versus the middle-class farmers and merchants. The real enemy of liberty in the valley, then, is not some distant crown in a remote imperial capital, but a group of haughty native aristocrats—represented most vividly in Frederic's novel by the malevolent Philip Cross—who threaten their easy-going, democratic-minded neighbors, including Douw Mauverensen, with the intolerable tyranny of class domination. The patriots of New York, Douw points out, are moved to battle for reasons quite different from those that urge the other colonies to rebel against England. It is the immediate fear of a brutal native aristocracy headed by Johnsons and Butlers, not "the more abstract and educated discontent of New England and Virginia" that motivates the patriots of *In the Valley,* many of whom (as their ablest leader, Nicholas Herkimer, points out) have had bitter experience enough with aristocracies in other lands. "If they try to make here another aristocracy over us," says Herkimer, speaking for his fellow farmers, "then we will die first before we will submit."

Douw himself, although he has been superficially touched by aristocratic tradition as he grows up in Mr. Stewart's house, takes his place early with his own social stock, and comes to manhood a thoroughgoing Whig. In Albany, where he nurses his chagrin at having lost Daisy to Philip Cross, Douw is surprised to learn that there is a Colony-wide storm brewing and that the unrest he had seen at home was not an isolated phenomenon. "Up in our slow, pastoral, uninformed Valley," he comments, "we rustics had been conscious of disturbances . . . but had lacked the skill and information—perhaps the interest as well—to interpret these signs of impending storm aright."

Word comes of the fighting in the eastern colonies and of General Washington's successes and failures. But

> the situation in the Valley was extremely simple. There was a small outspoken Tory party, who made no secret of their sympathies. . . . There was a somewhat larger Whig party, which by word and deed supported Congress. Between these two, or rather, because of their large number, surrounding them, was the great neutral party, who were chiefly concerned to so trim their sails that they should ship no water whichever way the wind blew.

An earlier generation of New Yorkers, in other words, is afflicted with the same kind of political apathy that Frederic had already condemned in their descendants, the public of *Seth's Brother's Wife*. But once more he demonstrates that the apathy can be dispelled and the quiet people can come dramatically alive under the leadership of one of their own number. As news comes back that the hated Tories, with their dreaded Indian allies, are approaching from the west with St. Leger's army of British regulars, the lethargic valley stirs under the prodding of the "rough, uneducated little frontier trader," Nicholas Herkimer, who has seen the issue all along and is prepared to meet it squarely in battle.

Frederic's lengthy and vivid description of the battle itself, "the fearsome death-struggle in the forest" near Oriskany—in his opinion the most crucial single event in New York history—is, properly, the high point of the novel. It constitutes the culminating chapter in which all the threads and themes of the story are brought together. Into his account of the bloody day's business Frederic poured all the enthusiasm for his task that had been stirring within him for almost a decade, all the knowledge he had acquired from his store of documents, and all the craftsmanship of romance that he had learned in the three years since he wrote "The Blakelys of Poplar Place." Marred only at the end by the implausibly motivated efforts of Douw to save his fallen enemy, Philip Cross, Frederic's account of Oriskany emerges as one of the most moving and convincing pictures of savage warfare in all of American historical romance. His long and patient plan to dramatize the story of how his own industrious, democratic, middle-class ancestors united on a day in 1777 to meet the threat of class tyranny is here finally and effectively realized.

Disagreeing with those New England historians who dismissed the battle of Oriskany as a minor skirmish that was at best a stalemate, Frederic believed that the issues of the Revolution as they directly affected upstate New York were settled by the determination of Herkimer and his bobtail citizens' army. Whatever happened afterward in the Revolution was, in a sense, anticlimactic so far as upstate New York was concerned. As Frederic saw it, the threat of class domination was destroyed at Oriskany; and the people won—as they win a less vivid struggle in *Seth's Brother's Wife*—because of the tough and honest fiber of a few strong leaders like Nicholas Herkimer, who stir their neighbors from an inertia that all too often characterizes a democratic society.

Considered simply as an account of an episode in American political and military history, then, *In the Valley* is successful. But Frederic was concerned with the social history of his valley as well, and so the novel abounds in authentic sidelights on the everyday life, customs, and traditions of the Mohawk Valley Germans and Dutch, in pre-Revolutionary days. Woven skillfully into the background, so that they become organically part of the fabric of the story, are Douw's reflections on such things as fur trading expeditions that are actually "coming-of-age" rituals, on the place of the Negro slave in colonial New York, on life in Albany when it was "almost as much in the wilderness as Caughnawaga." Not since the days of Cooper and James Kirke Paulding had life on the old Dutch-German frontier been recreated so carefully and lovingly.

For all its merits as dramatized history, however, *In the*

Valley is hardly the great novel—the American *Henry Esmond* —that Frederic had long dreamed of writing. From the very beginning, in fact, from the day in 1877 when the inspiration first came to his mind, *In the Valley* was predestined to questionable success, at best, as first-rate fiction. Through all the years of planning, and finally through the months of writing, Frederic was clearly more interested in the events of his story than in its characters. As a result, most of the fictional people in the novel (with the exception of occasional minor figures who are actually part of the setting) are too often mechanical, one-dimensional, and weakly motivated. Douw Mauverensen himself emerges as a character of some depth, although he sometimes talks like a device rather than like a human being. The others—Daisy, Philip Cross, Mr. Stewart—wear interesting costumes and move in the direction that the story demands; but they are not always convincingly real.

In the Valley, then, deserves praise as good reading, but not as distinguished fiction. Frederic himself seems to have been at least satisfied with what he had done in the novel, although he recommended it to President Cleveland with more restraint than he had used in writing about *Seth's Brother's Wife*. "It occurs to me," he wrote Cleveland on November 13, 1889,

> to beg you to try to see something at least of the story of mine now running in *Scribner's* called *In the Valley*. It is a close study of the rural part of our State during the Revolutionary period, full of patriotic color and impulse. . . . I myself have so great a liking for the political side that if I could be sure that every young man in the United States would read it, I should feel like working day and night to provide everyone of them with a free copy. I know that you don't read novels—but this is grave enough to be something else, and I shall doubt the wisdom of ever having written it if you don't read it."[7]

Whether or not Cleveland ever read this novel that was also "something else," another distinguished American certainly did, and found little in it to praise. Writing in *Harper's* for October, 1890, William Dean Howells sniffed at *In the Valley* as "a fresh instance of the fatuity of the historical novel as far as the portrayal of character goes." The book was "uncommonly well written," Howells admitted, but the characters were merely "persons of our own generation made up for the parts; well trained, well costumed, but actors, and almost amateurs."[8]

Had this sharp comment by the acknowledged dean of American letters appeared earlier, it would undoubtedly have stung Frederic deeply. By the time it was written, however, Frederic's third novel was already in print; and Howells' kind words for *The Lawton Girl,* as well as for *Seth's Brother's Wife,* made up at least in part for his lack of enthusiasm for *In the Valley.*

III *The Lawton Girl*

By June, 1887, before he had finished *In the Valley,* Frederic was already making carefully detailed notes for his third novel, *The Lawton Girl.* This work, he said later, "suggested itself at the outset as a kind of sequel to *Seth's Brother's Wife*";[1] it was to be, in other words, a second "contemporary story" about life in upstate New York as he himself had seen it.

Coming as it did at the very time he was completing a historical romance that he had anticipated writing for years, Frederic's decision to return to the contemporary scene in his third novel was significant. As his letter to Cleveland indicates, he was not dissatisfied with *In the Valley.* In that romance, furthermore, he had called upon only a small part of his impressive store of knowledge of New York history. It would have been a simple matter now to turn to other aspects of the Revolution, or of Mohawk Valley history, and to continue in other works the strain begun in *In the Valley.* When the urge came to write a sequel, why did he not write one to "the real work," the historical romance—or a series of sequels, in which he could revel to his heart's content in the social, political, and military history of New York? Why did he decide, instead, to return to realism (a term, incidentally, that Frederic seldom used) of the kind that characterizes *Seth's Brother's Wife*?

Although Frederic nowhere provides the answers to these questions, it seems reasonable to conjecture that the decision was deliberate: as he neared the end of *In the Valley,* he began to fret under the restrictions imposed upon him by the very nature of historical romance. By 1887 Frederic was too much a man of his own time, too alive to people and problems that he saw or had seen in the world about him, to be content with portraying dead worlds and costumed characters whose behavior must conform to the facts of history. By now, too, he had required a deep respect for William Dean Howells as a novelist and as a critical theorist. After hearing *The Rise of Silas Lapham* praised by a group of English readers after its appearance in 1885, Frederic had written to Howells that "they were not able to understand as well as I do, I think, how much more there is in the story—to realize that it means the scrutiny of a master turned for the first time upon what is the most distinctive phase of American folk life. . . ."[2] Now, having finished the one historical romance that he had long ago promised himself, he may have decided to follow Howells' example and to scrutinize thereafter distinctive phases of contemporary "American folk life."

Whatever his reasoning, Frederic was through with the full-length historical romance. He began *The Lawton Girl* at once and finished it a little more than a year later. In August, 1889, it was in Scribner's hands. Unlike his previous novels, *The Lawton Girl* was not first serialized in *Scribner's Magazine*; in 1890, it appeared in a fifty-cent paperback edition and in a conventional trade edition.

As he had previously done in *Seth's Brother's Wife,* Frederic unfolds in *The Lawton Girl* a fast-moving but complicated story with slightly daring overtones; this time, however, he uses a background which is in itself a dramatization of the conflict between two sharply different attitudes toward the forces of social Darwinism. As the novel opens, Jessica Lawton, the title character, is returning to her home village of Thessaly in upstate New York—the same village that figures in *Seth's Brother's Wife* and, later, in *The Damnation of Theron Ware*. She returns to the village in courageous shame having borne an illegitimate child whose father she is reluctant to identify. At one level, the novel is concerned with Jessica Lawton's subsequent efforts to re-establish herself in her small community by working out—like Hester Prynne—a course of penance which she designs for herself. This narrative thread soon gets all but lost, however, in the concurrent story of

Reuben Tracy, a "poor schoolmaster" in *Seth's Brother's Wife,* who has become a lawyer before the action of *The Lawton Girl* begins. This more important of the two plots, which are loosely connected by Jessica, dramatizes Tracy's exposure of dishonest financial manipulations which, if unchecked, would have upset the economy of the whole village.

Thessaly, which is representative of dozens of upstate villages in the post-Civil War years, depends heavily for its communal welfare on the successful operation of its one large industry, the Minster ironworks, which "had been built by one of the cleverest and most daring of all the strong men whom that section produced, the late Stephen Minster." The ironworks and a fortune "ranging somewhere between two and three millions of dollars" had by now devolved upon Minster's widow and two daughters. One of the daughters, Kate Minster, is a major character in the novel.

The same train that brings Jessica Lawton back to her village in disgrace also brings back, in a drawing-room car, the young man who had seduced her, Horace Boyce. Boyce is returning from a stay in Europe, where he had gone "to pursue more recondite studies . . . both in and out of his chosen profession of the law." No one in Thessaly but Jessica and her father, Ben Lawton—"a shiftless sort of coot who lives out in the hollow, and picks up odd jobs"—knows that the arrogant and pseudo-sophisticated young Boyce is the man in Jessica's past.

These four characters, all introduced quickly into the action, represent the vague distinctions of social class which have developed naturally in the days since Douw Mauverensen and his middle-class peers destroyed the threat of an idle aristocracy in battle on a slope only a few miles away from the Minster ironworks. Kate Minster (who is revealed as Douw Mauverensen's great-granddaughter) represents Thessaly's small and revered aristocracy of wealth—wealth gained by her father, whose memory hangs over the village as a symbol of vigorous enterprise. Reuben Tracy, as the novel opens, represents its middle class: intelligent, industrious, and honestly ambitious. Jessica Lawton is a daughter of the small lower class, doubly hampered in life by her own mistake and by her family's reputation in the village, which sees the

Lawtons as "the sort of people who were brought up on the canal and eat woodchucks." Horace Boyce, returning now to the village after an absence of several months, is, like Albert Fairchild in *Seth's Brother's Wife,* something of an outsider; when he does assume a position, however, it is somewhere between Kate Minster's and Reuben Tracy's. Boyce has college training, foreign experience, and a name that is still respected; all he lacks to put him in the Minster class is money—and this he intends to acquire by marrying Kate.

Behind the story involving these four characters, Frederic examines the fluidity of class which social commentators from de Tocqueville on have noted as being characteristic of American society. Reuben Tracy, a kind of "natural gentleman," moves freely across class lines with the aid of his own carefully developed qualities: intelligence, honesty, initiative. Kate Minster is his female counterpart with the added attributes of wealth and inherited social position. Together they recognize the moral emptiness of Horace Boyce, who, to Kate Minster, "looks precisely like all the other young men you see in New York nowadays," and who errs first when he tries to impress his decadent "fine gentlemen" ways on the community, and more seriously when he allows himself to be trapped in an unholy alliance.

Boyce, innocently at first, joins two unscrupulous speculators who have designs on the Minster properties and fortune. One of these, the actual villain of the piece, is a "mysterious New Yorker" named Wendover, whose predatory, robber-baron techniques threaten the industrial edifice erected by benevolent Stephen Minster and owned by the three respected Minster women. The third member of the group that threatens the community welfare is Schuyler Tenney, a local entrepreneur who looks "like any other of ten hundred hundreds of young Americans who are engaged in making more money than they need." Tenney is the apprentice robber-baron, learning the tricks from the master, Wendover.

The battle for the Minster ironworks soon occurs between two opposing forces: Reuben Tracy is on one side; Wendover, Tenney, and Boyce are on the other. What follows is an interesting, timely dramatization of the battle that was going on—even as Frederic was writing *The Lawton Girl*—between two irreconcilably opposed philosophies of social Darwinism. Frederic endows Wendover and Tenney with a crude, materialistic philosophy derived from William Graham Sumner's defense of unrestricted competition as a law of nature; he endows Reuben Tracy with a conflicting social philosophy derived from Lester Ward's attack on the premises of the prevailing *laissez-faire* philosophy. The outcome that Frederic assigns to the struggle—Tracy's victory is, in a sense, Ward's victory—provides insight into Frederic's social thinking and is consistent with his political and economic stands throughout his career not only as a novelist but also as a journalist.

Sumner's *What Social Classes Owe to Each Other,* a kind of manifesto of "hard" social Darwinism, had appeared in 1883 during Frederic's stay in Albany. In the same year had appeared Ward's *Dynamic Sociology,* in essence a defense of the necessity of government intervention in business and hence a denial of the validity of Sumner's theories. Even if he were not familiar at first-hand with these antithetical expressions of social doctrine, Frederic, as the socially-conscious editor of an important newspaper, could hardly have been unaware of the controversies that the two books had set off in newspapers and periodicals of the day. He could, for example, have gained a working knowledge of both Sumner's and Ward's ideas from reading, in the New York periodical *Man,* Ward's vigorously critical review of Sumner's *What Social Classes Owe to Each Other.*[3] In any case, by the time Frederic was writing *The Lawton Girl,* the implications behind the Sumner-Ward battle were in the air. As he looked back at the kind of struggles he had seen about him in Utica and Albany—struggles between ruthless, amoral (and often immoral) individuals on the one side and alert, socially-conscious area and regional leaders on the other—Frederic saw once more the stuff of which dramatic fiction can be made.

In *The Lawton Girl* Schuyler Tenney, who speaks also for Wendover, explicitly defends the extremes to which Sumner's doctrine of unrestricted competition might lead. His definition of business is simple and completely devoid of any ethical or moral implications: "All business," he points out, "consists in getting other people's money. . . . Everybody is looking out to get rich; and when a man succeeds, it only means that somebody else has got poor. That's plain common-sense." And when Horace Boyce, curious about his own role in Tenney's plans to acquire the Minster holdings, asks him: "Broadly, what do you propose?" Tenney answers:

> "Broadly, what does everybody propose? To get for himself what somebody else has got. That's human nature. It's every kind of nature, down to the little chickens just hatched who start to chase the chap with the worm in his mouth before they've fairly got their tails out of the shell."

To this Sumnerian observation, Horace answers in jest: "You ought to write a book. . . . 'Tenney on Dynamic Sociology'!" —a suggestion which is either irony or error, since "dynamic sociology" was Ward's term for his own theories as contrasted with Sumner's. But regardless of mistaken terminology, Boyce drifts willingly into the orbit of Tenney and Wendover, telling himself that "the case was too complicated for mere honesty" and that "to eat others was the rule now, if one would save himself from being devoured."

Reuben Tracy, meanwhile, has been developing along very different lines—as a social planner and potential trustbuster—in the direction of Lester Ward's theory of purposeful social activity, or "collective telesis." His plan for a village society "made up of men who have an interest in the town and who want to do good" is a step in the direction of what Ward called "sociocracy": the planned control of society by society as a whole. Through the organized efforts of the whole community, Tracy hopes, the village of Thessaly can cure its own ills: "the greed for money, the drunkenness, the indifference to real education, the neglect of health," and other social evils. Jessica Lawton and Kate Minster, too—far apart as their social positions are—share Tracy's convictions and join in plans for "a sort of evening club for the working-girls of the town," a project which Tracy actively encourages.

Tracy's great triumph comes when he exposes the ramifications of the swindle that "Wendover and some of the heads of the pig-iron trust" had planned—a swindle which, had it succeeded, would have crippled the economy of the village and destroyed the stability which was a testimonial to the late Stephen Minster's "unostentatious, useful career." And Tracy, aware of the issues that have been met and resolved, contemplates his achievement like a true "sociocrat":

> The triumph had its splendid public side. . . . Great and lasting good must follow such an exposure as he would make of the economic and social evils underlying the system of trusts. A staggering blow would be dealt to the system, and to the sentiment back of it that rich men might do what they liked in America. With pardonable pride he thrilled at the thought that his arm was to strike the blow. The effect would be felt all over the country.

As a novel, *The Lawton Girl* is not so well constructed as *Seth's Brother's Wife*. The first novel has a compactness of organization, a unity and coherence, that *The Lawton Girl* lacks. As the author himself pointed out later, his characters "took matters into their own hands quite from the start. . . . I grew so interested in the doings of these people that I lost sight of a time-limit." Jessica Lawton's death-scene in the final chapter, remarkable for its use of interior monologue and a curious mixture of pre-Freudian symbolism, is a gratuitous addition to the finished story. "At the end I did . . . kill Jessica," Frederic admitted, "she who had not deserved or intended at all to die—but I see now more clearly than anyone else that it was a false and cowardly thing to do."[4] All in all, *The Lawton Girl* is the most discursive and disorganized of Frederic's works, reflecting neither the long immersion in his background material that characterizes *In the Valley* nor the ability to stick to a clearly-defined plot like that of *Seth's Brother's Wife*.

Despite its faulty structure, *The Lawton Girl* is nevertheless the most ambitious of the first three novels that came in untiring succession from Frederic's pen. In it he attempted to cope with the same tremendous problem that has engaged social critics from Carlyle on—"the problem," as Walter F. Taylor defines it, "of assimilating into a previously existent humane culture the disruptive forces of capitalistic industrialism."[5] *The Lawton Girl* is Frederic's attempt to show the concrete manifestations of these forces as they operated within the very particular and specific framework of his own region. Theorists could talk abstractly about the dangers of industrialism in terms of Herbert Spencer's "Synthetic Philosophy" or John Fiske's "Cosmic Philosophy," or to take sides in William Graham Sumner's "holy war" against reformism, socialism, and government interventionism, or to look hopefully to the melioristic "dynamic sociology" of Lester Ward or the modified utilitarianism of men like E. L. Godkin. Frederic, however, saw the problem in the simple and concrete terms of a central New York village whose whole way of life is endangered when a group of scoundrels threaten to take over control of an ironworks.

In *Seth's Brother's Wife,* this same region had triumphed over political corruption; in *In the Valley* it had destroyed the threat of class tyranny; now, in *The Lawton Girl,* the region wins again—this time over economic despotism of the kind that Frederic saw to be inherent in the belief of social Darwinists like William Graham Sumner that "the social order is fixed by laws of nature precisely analogous to those of the physical order."[6] And all three victories had been achieved under the leadership of men who were themselves able and intelligent products of the region.

IV *The Return of the O'Mahony*

After the publication of *The Lawton Girl,* Frederic might have been expected to continue without interruption the exploitation of his "native heath" as a background for his stories. He was not yet to abandon it, as his tales of the Civil War and his great work, *The Damnation of Theron Ware,* later proved. But his nearly seven years away from the Mohawk Valley and the expanding of his environmental as well as his intellectual horizons brought other faces and other scenes into the foreground of his thinking.

In one of the three appointment diaries that remain among Frederic's papers, that of 1891 bears his notation of February 2: "Began Irish Novel." On October 24 of the same year he sent the manuscript of *The Return of the O'Mahony* to his publishers. Meanwhile, he had commenced a long series of articles for the *National Observer* in London: "Observations in Philistia," which he collected and published under the title *Mrs. Albert Grundy* in 1892. He had finished his biography of

William II of Germany and had sent it to the printers on May 20. It was published on July 6. From April 12 until April 24 he had spent two happy weeks in Ireland, fishing and visiting many of the scenes that became the backdrop for his characters in the Irish novel. And for three weeks, from July 23 until August 14, he traveled in Russia—from St. Petersburg to Moscow and from Kiev to Odessa, and other places—collecting data for his articles to the *Times* that later were to appear in a book called *The New Exodus,* a firsthand report about the Jewish pogrom under Alexander III, the next to the last of the Russian czars. The year 1891 was a busy and productive one for Harold Frederic.

Moreover, if *The Return of the O'Mahony* is any criterion, it was a year filled with laughter, with a sense of accomplishment, and with that robustiousness which one finds in his hero, Zeke Tisdale, The O'Mahony of this delightful fiction. When we first see him, Zeke, regarded as the "father of Company F," is preparing to fight in one of the last battles of the Civil War. But through a chain of circumstances at once highly improbable and altogether plausible, he confiscates papers intended for another member of his company, deserts the army, and goes to Ireland to claim the inheritance of the O'Mahony estates. Thereafter complications rise for Zeke, and many others besides, that make this novel one of the most readable comedies of the period.

In all, Frederic depended chiefly upon character, language, and situation to achieve his comic effect. Probably no other American could have represented so faithfully both the Irish character and dialect as he created them for this, his gayest book; for few men were as admirably equipped with Frederic's intimate knowledge of all things Irish. He could call up his experiences with Father Terry, with the McQuades, with John Howe, and doubtless with hundreds of other Irish men and women in Utica. As a proponent of the Irish Land League and Home Rule movements, he had come to know many of the influential Irish members of Parliament, among these a few who were to introduce him to Ireland itself and to the problems with which the Irish were confronted. More significantly still they made it possible for him very early in his career as London correspondent of the *Times* to visit

Ireland and to meet its people. Even as he wrote this novel, it should be remembered, he traveled again the route from Queenstown (now Cobh) to the O'Mahony castles, to Dunmanus Bay, and other spots in Cork that become a familiar part of *The Return of the O'Mahony.*

Though it is true that Frederic notes with some unhappiness the sad condition of the Irish peasant, that he reveals the folly of the Fenian movement in which Zeke Tisdale becomes involved, and that he comments upon certain weaknesses in the Irish nature, he does not fail to maintain an essentially comic spirit throughout the narrative. From the very outset, Zeke commands the interest and later the approval of the reader: Zeke, neither Irish nor Catholic, is an anomaly; he must discover how to make himself over into an Irishman and, what is more important, must be the image of The O'Mahony, the lord of the manor. For a man who has spent most of his adult life soldiering, this accomplishment calls for a remarkable metamorphosis. But Zeke is equal to the transmutation: he fairly bulges out of his cocoon to become the greatest in many a generation to bear the nine-hundred-year-old name.

In his appointment book for April 12, 1891, Frederic jotted down the following route: "Dublin at 7; Mail train to Queenstown; lunch and 30 miles drive with Jerry." And so it is for Zeke Tisdale: in the novel he arrives at Queenstown, finds a cab driver by the name of Jerry Higgins, installs Jerry as his guide and personal servant, and goes with him to the O'Mahony castle. Jerry acquaints Zeke with Irish ways and speech; Jerry also takes him to "all the masses there are in Cork" because Zeke plainly does not know even the first word of his "Christian obligations." Jerry was, in fact, a very real Irishman. As Barry Forman tells us, he was still driving a "side-car or a jaunting-car" probably as late as the last year of Frederic's life, when Frederic, Kate, and their children took a vacation in Ireland.

Once Zeke and Jerry reach Dunmanway, however, they meet Cormac O'Daly, hereditary bard of the O'Mahonys of Muirisc, who begins almost at once to regale Zeke with a poem composed for the celebrated return of the O'Mahony. O'Daly is a "diminutive man, past middle age, dressed in a costume which The O'Mahony [Zeke] had seen once or twice on the stage but never before in every-day life." The meeting is characteristic of Frederic's whimsical humor.

> "Is it The O'Mahony of Muirisc that I have the honor to see before me?" [O'Daly] asked, his little ferret eyes dividing their glances between the two.
>
> "I'm your huckleberry," said The O'Mahony, and held out his hand.
>
> The small man bent his shriveled form double in salutation, and took the proffered hand with ceremonious formality.
>
> "Sir, you're kindly welcome back to your ancesthral domain," he said, with an emotional quaver in his thin, high voice. "All your people are waitin' with anxiety and pleasure for the sight of your face."
>
> "I hope they've got us somethin' to eat," said The O'Mahony. "We had breakfast at daybreak this morning, so's to work the churches, and I'm . . ."
>
> "His honor," hastily interposed Jerry, "is that pious he can't sleep of a mornin' for pinin' to hear mass."

One is struck by the puckish nature of Frederic's comic image. Jerry Higgins and Cormac O'Daly are a pair of leprechauns. Jerry is a good fellow, loyal, devoted, completely trustworthy; Cormac O'Daly, as it develops during The O'Mahony's long exile, is a pompous little scamp who usurps The O'Mahony's position and all but destroys the good work the American had done not only for the estate but also for the peasantry who depend upon it for a livelihood. These two seemingly represented for Frederic the two faces of Ireland: the one simple, ignorant, the willing servant of a good master; the other shrewd, not over-scrupulous, stubbornly clinging to the old ways.

Zeke Tisdale, once installed as The O'Mahony, has in any case to live with both men. When he arrives at the O'Mahony castle, he finds that what once was greatness is now only ruins. He discovers to his dismay that the only really inhabitable portion is a "small, square chamber, roofed with blackened oak beams, and having arched doors and windows. Its walls, partly of stone, partly of plaster roughly scratched," are whitewashed. The sanded floor is bare, save "for a cowskin mat spread before the fire." Ruins, then, are the "ancestral abode of the O'Mahonys of Muirisc," as O'Daly tells him and then explains:

> "There's this part of the castle that's inhabitable, and there's a part of the convent forninst the porch where the nuns live, but there's more of both, not to mintion the church, that's ruined entirely. Whatever your taste in ruins may plase to be, there'll be something to delight you. We have thim that's a thousand years old, and thim that's fallen into disuse since only last winter. Anny kind you like: Early Irish, pray-Norman, posht-Norman, Elizabethan, Georgian, or very late Victorian—here the ruins are for you, the natest and the most complate and convanient altogether to be found in Munster."

"So this is my ranch, eh?" The O'Mahony comments.

The convent mentioned houses three nuns of the order of the Ladies of the Hostage's Tears which had been founded in 1191. Since that time, the daughters of The O'Mahonys—those that have not married, at any rate—have joined this order. Three older women who carry on the tradition hope little Kate O'Mahony, a child of seven years, will keep the order alive. But The O'Mahony, believing that Kate would probably rather be "whoopin' round barefoot, with a nanny-goat . . . climbin' trees an' huntin' eggs . . . than go into partnership with grandma . . . in the nun business," whispers to Kate as he trots her on his knees: "Now don't you fret your gizzard, siss. . . , you needn't be a nun for one solitary darned minute, if you don't want to be." Many situations of rich comedy follow involving Mrs. Fergus O'Mahony, Kate's mother; Mother Agnes, the superior in her order; Jerry Higgins; Cormac O'Daly; and other characters connected with the household.

The Fenian adventure, however, holds the reader's attention chiefly in the first two-thirds of the narrative and is significant in the development of the plot of the whole novel. For The O'Mahony, undertaking with bravado a small rebellion against the British, only half succeeds in his mission and is forced into an exile that keeps him away from Ireland for twelve years. During that time, Kate grows into young womanhood and meets and falls in love with a young American mining engineer who, the reader soon learns, is the son of the true heir of the O'Mahony estates. During that time, too, O'Daly usurps the right of heirship, re-establishes the rents that The O'Mahony had reduced for the poor peasants on his land, evicts those who cannot meet their debts, allows a canning industry that The O'Mahony had built to go out of existence. In short, he falls back upon the customs of the ancient Irish master, and the good works of the American pretender are destroyed. Nevertheless, when The O'Mahony returns a second time, matters arrange themselves happily, as they should in a comedy. O'Daly is put in his place and humbled; Kate will marry Bernard O'Mahony; Zeke Tisdale, who was an impostor, remains the much beloved O'Mahony but announces that when he dies the title will rest on young Bernard.

The temptation rises—and it is a hard one to resist—to look at Frederic's *Fortnightly Review* articles written more than two years after *The Return of the O'Mahony* and to find in them the thesis for the Irish novel.[1] Mr. Haines contends that "the gayest of [Frederic's] novels is also his most carefully integrated fictional statement of a political thesis."[2] Mr. Woodward maintains that the thesis is contained in the conclusion of the last of these articles: "that the logical outcome of Home Rule must be the reconstruction of Ireland upon distinctly Irish lines."[3] The parallels are close enough to warrant some reading backward in the history of Frederic's intellectual development.

For it is true that it took Zeke Tisdale, an American using American business methods, to bring the O'Mahony properties once again into a flourishing state. And it is equally true that while he is in exile and O'Daly has taken over the authority, the properties deteriorate rapidly—and the peasants along with them. Kate deplores the "Great O'Daly Usurpation" and all that it has meant to the Ireland that she loves. The Fenian insurrection on which Zeke embarks, having been led into it by Jerry Higgins, is a reasonably close portrayal of the abortive attempts at rebellion made by Irish loyalists. That one Irishman betrays the plot and causes the British officer captured by The O'Mahony to comment, "There's always an Irishman who sells the secret to the government"—all this does in fact point to the possibility that Frederic was using his Irish novel as a political tract. One might almost say that the O'Mahony ruins become a symbol of the ruinous plight in which Frederic found the whole of Ireland and that his narrative is an instrument of propaganda.

But in the extant notes for both the novel and the uncompleted play version one can find not a single item suggesting such an interest or intent in Frederic's mind. The notes are scanty; but they reveal primarily a concern with organization of detail and with a delineation of basic conflicts between characters. On one page of the notes for the novel, Frederic even argues with himself about certain actions. "Have young Bernard O'Mahony kidnaped by watchful Murphy, to prevent what they believe be his felonious designs. Hidden with Linsky —or has Linsky died? Perhaps Murphy helped bury Linsky and so knows place. Or it might be O'Daly. Or there might be another chamber, adjoining Linsky's, secret of which O'Daly knows." Frederic did not, finally, utilize any of these possible plans; but they disclose an author at work, concerned particularly with the proper plotting of his narrative.

Frederic had, as has been suggested, often been in Ireland. He had in fact made a visit there as early as 1884. He was personally and vitally interested in Irish affairs and an active participant in what he considered a *cause célèbre.* Early in 1886 he talked with Tim Healy, one of the best known and most influential of the Irish members of Parliament, about getting the signatures of the eighty-five Irish representatives on a single sheet of paper; and, as he wrote to John Howe, he suggested that he might bring such a paper back to Utica with him on his expected vacation. "Would it be valued, do you think?" he wrote. "And, if it would not make too much trouble, I think I should like to meet your Branch, when I come, and make them a little talk on the subject."[4] At this point in his career he was assuredly enthusiastic about Ireland's chances for independence. He had by no means lost his enthusiasm when he wrote his O'Mahony comedy. But it is probable that by the time he came to write the *Fortnightly* articles he had suffered some disenchantment with Irish affairs generally. Two years had passed; the Irish cause had experienced reverses despite Mr. Gladstone's efforts on Home Rule; Frederic's ideas and attitudes had unquestionably undergone some changes, too.

Besides, he made Ireland a vacation land. He observed carefully whatever he saw and could surely be counted on to note and record the deplorable conditions that he found in Ireland, but he went there nonetheless in a holiday mood. He would as quickly see the comic as he would the tragic in Irish life. In the very midst of his writing of *The Return of the O'Mahony,* as we have said, he spent two weeks in Cork, more than likely taking Kate Lyon with him. Only the year before he and Kate had met and fallen in love. Now "Kate" became his heroine's name; and as Kate Lyon's mother had been an O'Mahony, he found special delight in learning all he could about the O'Mahonys of Muirisc.

The essential conflict in the novel is of course between the ancient and the modern; but if the political and social aspects of Irish life are part of the framework, they are, nevertheless, incidental. Frederic would surely have chosen a better vehicle than comedy had he wished to treat seriously what he recognized as serious problems.

V *The Civil War Stories*

At first reading, the seven stories of the American Civil War that Frederic produced in 1892 and 1893 would seem to have little connection with the recently completed comedy, *The Return of the O'Mahony.* The stories are completely different from the novel in purpose and tone and in locale and length. And yet, in at least one way, the realistic and sometimes somber stories grew directly out of the Irish novel.

In January, 1891, when he had cast about for a suitable way to start *O'Mahony,* Frederic had settled upon a happy device: in order to give the farcical plot some credibility, he had set the opening scenes amid the confusion of a Civil War battlefield. Furthermore, the real O'Mahony, the dead Union soldier who was the proper heir to an ancient Irish estate, is identified as having been a shoemaker in "Tecumsy"; and Zeke Tisdale, the unprincipled (at this stage) rascal who steals papers that give him a new identity is a reluctant soldier of fortune from northern New York.

Except for the brief opening chapters *The Return of the O'Mahony* has nothing, to be sure, to do with the Civil War. Nevertheless, when Frederic finished the Irish romance later in 1891, his thoughts seem to have turned almost immediately to new possibilities for fiction inherent in situations like the one with which he had opened the book. Although he had not participated in the Civil War, he, as a small boy in Utica, had seen its effects on the lives of friends and neighbors hundreds of miles away from the firing lines. It was not necessary, he remembered now, for one to go to war in order to be hurt; the war could hurt one apparently safe on a Utica street or an Oneida County farm.

Having uncovered a new, rich mine of fictional possibilities as he wrote *The O'Mahony*, Frederic began early in 1892 "to paint some small pictures of life in my Valley, under the shadow of the vast black cloud which was belching fire and death on its southern side." Most of the seven stories, he said, "are in a large part my own reflections of the dreadful time—the actual things that a boy from five to nine saw and heard about him, while his own relatives were being killed, and his school-fellows orphaned, and women of his neighborhood forced into mourning and despair—and they had a right to be recorded."[1]

In order to "record" these "actual things" effectively, Frederic once more utilized devices that he had admired in Erckmann-Chatrian, the French literary idols of his younger days. The stories, he admitted, were written "in humble imitation of their studies of Alsatian life in the days of the Napoleonic terror."[2] By using the simple Erckmann-Chatrian device of showing through the eyes of ingenuous narrators (usually a young boy) the effects of war on a civilian population affected by a conflict but not really a part of it, Frederic figuratively lifted up the faraway Civil War and set it down again in the middle of Oneida County.

"The Copperhead," actually a short novel, is the story of Abner Beech, a flint-minded conservative Democrat who is unhappily surrounded by Abolitionist neighbors of the type that had made Frederic's native county an anti-slavery battleground. When the course of events turns "Jee Hagadorn" and other "tiresome fanatics" of the fifties into the "inspired prophets" of the sixties, Abner Beech is left alone with his Copperhead principles—alone to battle against the cordon of distrust and anger that tightens around him in this New York countryside gone mad with the horrifying casualty lists that bring the destruction of far-off Antietam into the homes of "Dearborn County" farmers.

But the old Copperhead Beech bears both insult and violence with dignity—even the defection of his son who enlists in the ranks of what Abner Beech considers the unholy cause of the Union. Abner Beech defies his once respectful but now alienated neighbors and clings to his unpopular principles; the agony he consequently suffers does not swerve him, but it does teach him a humility that he lacked before. "The Copperhead" is Frederic's tribute to that considerable body of central New Yorkers who feared the hysterical and irrational elements inherent in the cause of the North and who refused with moral sincerity to embroil themselves in what they considered to be a useless and illegal attack on the property rights of other American citizens.

In his other "small pictures" Frederic explores with the calm perspective given by time the motives behind various aberrant actions during the nerve-straining war days. "The Deserter" represents a reversal of the usual story in which the folks at home worry about the welfare of the boy in uniform; in this story Mose Whipple, the drafted substitute, worries about his indigent father, helpless and alone on a patch of land back in central New York. Mose's desertion is prompted, not by cowardice and disloyalty to the Union, but by loyalty to his father, who needs his help at home. This fact is recognized by everyone concerned, including the marshall assigned to hunting Mose down. A writer like Ambrose Bierce would have reveled in the ironic possibilities of this situation; but Frederic was not an ironist like Bierce or Stephen Crane; and "The Deserter," like "The Copperhead," ends on a happy note.

Into these and other stories Frederic wove as part of the fictional fabric "the actual things that a boy from five to nine" had seen and heard in an upstate New York community while a distant war was changing the lives of the people around him: Marsena, the mild, artistic village photographer, goes to death in the War at the urging, not of patriotism or principle, but of a brainless village belle. Aunt Em Jones, the "War Widow," is doubly hurt when the death in the war of her colorless but beloved husband is cruelly overlooked in the family's grief for the death of Em's promising half-brother. Miss Stratford, the schoolteacher, receives erroneous word during the excitement of "The Eve of the Fourth" that her lover has been killed in battle.

These stories about various aspects of home life in his part of the North during the war were, according to Frederic, his favorite works. They were, he said, "by far closer to my heart than any other work of mine, partly because they seem to me to contain the best things I have done or ever shall do, partly because they are so closely interwoven with the personal memories and experiences of my own childhood—and a little also, no doubt, for the reason that they have not had quite the treatment outside that paternal affection had desired for them."[3]

Although the Civil War stories failed to attract critical attention, as Frederic's mild complaint implies, they were not without important admirers. Stephen Crane, for example, who usually had little to say about other authors' work, had high praise for *In the Sixties,* which contained five of the stories. "At about the time of the appearance of these stories," wrote Crane, "the critics were making a great deal of noise in an attempt to stake the novelists down to the soil and make them write the impressive common life of the United States." But even as the critics were clamoring, Crane continued, "There was Frederic doing his locality . . . with the strong hand of a great craftsman, and the critics were making such a din over the attempt to have a certain kind of thing done, that they did not recognize its presence."[4]

The Civil War stories continued to occupy Frederic through 1893 and the first part of 1894. But even before he had written the last of them, "A Day in the Wilderness," his deeper attention had turned to something else. His appointment book for 1893 contains a cryptic but significant sequence of entries. "June 19," it says, "Gave Marsena to typewriter. 18,900 words." Then, "August 16. Wed.: Brandon—beginning of Maddens."[5]

Already, in other words, the characters of *The Damnation of Theron Ware* were taking shape in his mind. Frederic was occupied with a novel that would bring him more than enough acclaim to make up for the neglect of his "small pictures" about the Civil War days of his boyhood.

CHAPTER 5

The Damnation of Theron Ware

IN OCTOBER, 1896, an unknown young poet in Gardiner, Maine, wrote to a friend, "You make me uncomfortable with your talk about *Illumination.* I have not read the book, but, if I am to believe half that I read about it, it must be a bigger thing than I am ever likely to put my name to."[1] The book that Edwin Arlington Robinson had read about was Harold Frederic's new novel, which had been published in England in February as *Illumination* and a month later in America as *The Damnation of Theron Ware.* Robinson's comment provides an accurate, if indirect, reflection of the enthusiasm with which reviewers and critics, especially in England, were still writing six months after its publication about Frederic's third, full-length study of contemporary life in upstate New York. *The Damnation of Theron Ware,* a number of them vigorously agreed in articles and notices of the kind that Robinson had seen, was the most exciting novel of the publishing year.

In April, 1896, six weeks after its London publication, the book was already something of a sensation in England. "It is a long time, I fancy, since any novel has achieved success among so many classes of readers as Mr. Harold Frederic's *Illumination,"* wrote Arthur Waugh. "[He] seems to have caught both critic and public in a single throw of his net."[2] Weeks later, the American edition was receiving some awe-tinged praise. *The Damnation of Theron Ware,* said an anonymous reviewer in *The Critic,* is "a tremendously impressive study, positively painful in its intensity, of the development of a human soul."[3]

Harry Thurston Peck, one of America's most respected critics, was so impressed that he praised the book in two different reviews. "*The Damnation of Theron Ware* is distinctly a great novel," he said flatly in the June *Bookman.*[4] Two months later, in *Cosmopolitan,* he carefully explained and defended his judgment. After pointing out that only "three or four" authors had successfully accomplished the task of writing truly American novels, Peck asserted that "Mr. Frederic has very certainly accomplished it with his vivid, strong, and masterful delineation of a corner of American life as it actually is—the good and the bad, the fine and the crude, the enlightened and the ignorant—in one finely drawn, consistent picture imbued with penetrating power." The publication of a book like *The Damnation of Theron Ware,* Peck concluded, "is a literary event of great importance."[5]

In England, wrote Israel Zangwill in September, Harold Frederic had "set the Thames on fire with his *Illumination.* . . . It is only not a good novel, but a good novel of the best kind."[6] Some reviews, to be sure, fell far short of the general enthusiasm; but these did not dull the edge of the initial excitement about the book. But had it appeared on the market at a time when realistic novels were approved throughout the land, it probably would have made an even deeper impression on the contemporary literary scene.

Despite the tastes of the era and because of its critical acclaim, *The Damnation of Theron Ware* sold from the day it first appeared and for some months in impressive quantities. By June 1, the publishers, Stone and Kimball, were finding it difficult to supply the demand.[7] When Edwin Arlington Robinson wistfully scanned the latest reviews, hoping in vain to find a friendly notice of his first volume of poetry, *Ware* was near the top of every list of best-sellers reported in America for October, 1896. Readers across America, from Atlanta to Portland, Oregon, from Boston to Los Angeles, were demanding copies of Frederic's book.[8]

I

It is a much simpler task to trace the immediate success of *The Damnation of Theron Ware* (or *Illumination,* as it continued to be called in England) than to discover its genesis in Frederic's mind. Earlier in his career, as an eager apprentice-novelist, he had been quick to inform his friends about his progress with *Seth's Brother's Wife,* with *In the Valley,* and even with *The Lawton Girl.* But as the subtleties and complexities of *Ware* came to him—elating or discouraging him, as the case may have been—he stored them away and confided in no one. *Ware* was to be a product of a side of Frederic's mind that the world had not yet seen: a brooding, introspective side, pondering in solitude the "mysterious, impersonal, Titanic forces" that a perceptive reviewer later spoke of as hovering over the novel.[9]

The Damnation of Theron Ware, from the very beginning, was not to be discussed except in his own notes. Year after year, as these notes became more and more voluminous and almost incredibly detailed and as Frederic himself coped with a bewildering array of pressing journalistic, editorial, and domestic responsibilities, the young minister who eventually faced the world as Theron Ware walked slowly and inexorably to his doom in the secret recesses of Harold Frederic's mind.

Vague plans for *Ware* had occurred to Frederic perhaps as far back as his Utica days when his long conversations with Father Terry, the brilliant and candid priest, had so stimulated him. By October, 1890—shortly after publication of *In the Valley* and *The Lawton Girl*—the idea for the novel was clear enough for him to write three different versions of a tentative "Prologue," which he eventually discarded, and to assemble a cast of characters, which included a number who never appeared in the finished novel.[10]

But *The Damnation of Theron Ware* is more than a product of five years of conscious, careful, and silent planning; it is in some ways the result of Frederic's whole life up to 1895. Into it he poured nearly everything that he had learned about human strength and frailty in almost forty years of living. And since the germ for the novel had been planted in some way in his mind by the words and behavior of a Roman Catholic priest, the characters and the story itself grew naturally against a background of religion as he had seen it in his native Utica through the days of his boyhood and young manhood. As one contemporary reviewer pointed out, *The Damnation of Theron Ware* is "by no means a 'religious' or controversial novel." It is, instead, as he went on to say, "a 'human document'—the story of a little earthenware pot which goes to swim gaily among the stronger vessels, and is broken by the way."[11] Theron Ware's "damnation" is intellectual and moral, as well as religious; but it is more dramatic and vivid because it occurs within a religious context.

Long before he started to write *Ware*, Frederic was impressed by the variety of ways in which the foundations of the religious orthodoxy of his parents' home were being sapped not by mere scoffers or by partisans who wrote from their own sectarian viewpoints but by discriminating thinkers who included not only biological scientists but even some widely respected clergymen. Since Frederic had worn his own religious training lightly for many years, not the attacks themselves on religious orthodoxy but their variety impressed him. Everywhere he turned in his wide reading he found different avenues of assault on the kind of religion that his mother's circle back in Utica had found so comfortable. Some of the assaults were direct, albeit disinterested, like those of the post-Darwinian scientists; others were oblique, like the calm pronouncements of the apostles of the so-called "higher criticism"—scholars who discussed the Bible as if it were just another book; and still others were camouflaged, their disturbing implications half-hidden beneath a rich veneer of aestheticism, like the artistic reactions of Ruskin and the pre-Raphaelites, and especially the intellectual epicureanism of Walter Pater and his followers. By 1890 Frederic was well aware that one who entered the modern lists equipped only with the thin defensive armor of primitive Methodism was in grave intellectual and spiritual danger.

Although Frederic could watch the attack on ancient orthodoxies with appreciative detachment, he remembered the beginnings of his own "illumination"—his first significant exposure to spiritual traditions other than the one that had descended to him from John Wesley and Lorenzo Dow and he could hardly help wondering how he might have fared under other conditions. How *did* the religious innocent of the time, confident of his own spiritual security, meet the sudden, many-pronged invasions of a religious and intellectual *terra firma* whose impregnability he had not only taken for granted but had also been persuading others to accept without question? How would the "illumination"—which Frederic had been able to take in stride—affect, for instance, a sincere but intellectually provincial young man who had been formally trained to preach the very orthodoxies that were now being undermined by forces of whose existence he was not even aware? Frederic concluded that what had resulted in true "illumination" for him might well result in a spiritual downfall—a kind of damnation—for another.

As the tragic plight of such an innocent caught in a spiritual revolution grew on Frederic, he began to see the universal implications once more in the concrete terms of his own familiar Oneida County. As early as 1892 in "Cordelia and the Moon" he had glanced contemplatively at one dim facet of the religious life of the central New York of his boyhood. Into this story he had introduced not only a rebellious and beautiful young church organist but also a minister named Ware and a group of ultra-conservative church members who were more concerned with trifling foibles than with real moral and spiritual problems. Into *The Lawton Girl* of 1890 he had introduced very tentatively a minor character he called Father Chance, the Catholic priest of Thessaly, "a broad-shouldered, athletic young man, who preached very commonplace sermons but did an enormous amount of pastoral work." With these three characters as a foundation, Frederic went ahead with his story of Theron Ware, the eager but intellectually callow minister who disintegrates morally before the "mysterious, impersonal, Titanic forces" whose real significance is hidden behind the amiable and stimulating personalities of a Catholic priest, a hoydenish Irish organist, and a sophisticated non-practicing physician who professes atheism. Once more, but this time in what is undoubtedly a "there-but-for-the-grace-of-God" story, Frederic brought abstract, universally disruptive world-ideas to the seemingly provincial confines of his native city in upstate New York as he traced the destruction of a young minister by inscrutable forces that he innocently stirred up in the very shadow of his church steeple.

The village of Octavius, in which Theron Ware suffers his damnation, is a carefully representative Mohawk Valley town of the 1870's. The village population is neatly divided into two segments: a large "native American" group with occasionally discernible New England roots; and a smaller but very considerable body of first and second generation Irish who are gradually assuming characteristics of the middle class. Other nationalities are mentioned—the "Eyetalians" who work in the stone quarries, for example—but do not figure significantly in village affairs.

After establishing the entire population as a frame of reference, Frederic focuses his attention on two small groups within the two main segments. He reveals the narrowest level of primitive, almost fundamentalist, members of Theron Ware's Methodist congregation of "native Americans"; and he depicts the other extreme, the broadest level, through two of the Irish: Father Forbes and Celia Madden. Theron Ware's people, in other words, are members of the extremely conservative wing of a traditionally liberal religious tradition; Father Forbes and Celia, on the other hand, are members of the extremely liberal wing of a traditionally conservative religious tradition. The intellectual gulf between the two groups is, therefore, well-nigh unbridgeable. Dr. Ledsmar, another character who figures in Theron Ware's "damnation," is a scientist rather than a practicing physician; and he serves as a kind of chorus character who is appropriately detached from both groups. Although he admires Father Forbes, he has little love for either Celia Madden or Theron Ware's dour congregation.

In these groups and in the isolated character of Ledsmar, who comments disinterestedly on both, Frederic draws a vivid, concentrated picture of the extremes of spiritual attitudes and development within the organized Christianity of his region in the crucial 1870's and 1880's. These extremes are best exemplified in the contrasting attitudes toward religion of Father Forbes and Loren Pierce, a trustee of Theron Ware's church. Pierce, informing the young Methodist minister of what will be expected of him in Octavius, declares:

> "We are a plain sort o' folks up in these parts. . . . We ain't gone traipsin' after strange gods like some people that call themselves Methodists in other places. . . . We don't want no book-learning' or dictionary words in our pulpit. . . . What we want here, sir, is straight-out, flat-footed hell—and the

> burnin' lake o' fire an' brimstone. Pour it into 'em, hot an' strong. . . . And then, too, our folks don't take no stock in all that pack o' nonsense about science, such as telling the age of the earth by crackin' up stones. I've been in the quarry all my life, an' *I* know it's all humbug."

Shortly after hearing this declaration from one of his trustees, Theron Ware listens uncomfortably as Father Forbes talks learnedly about "the original prototype of our 'divine intermediary' idea" and "whole receding series of types of this Christ-myth of ours."

Somewhere between the two extremes exists the great majority of the people of Octavius, both "native American" and Irish, who are not deeply concerned with matters of either the spirit or the intellect. Frederic, in turn, is not concerned with them. *The Damnation of Theron Ware,* unlike his other New York novels, is not primarily a study of a society, but of the unsuccessful attempt of an individual to move from one intellectual level of that society to another; it is, as Everett Carter has observed, "the story of the fall of a man, rather than his salvation, through illumination and knowledge."[12] But the very fact that such illumination and knowledge are available to Theron Ware a mere step beyond the boundaries of his own relatively benighted parish is also an important part of the story.

Father Forbes as a type is new only to Theron Ware's heretofore restricted vision. In a sense the direct descendant of Montaigne and Sir Thomas Browne, Forbes is a latter-day fideist of whom it might be said, as Basil Willey has said of Browne, that he has "the capacity to live in divided and distinguished worlds, and to pass freely to and fro between one and another." He is equally at ease at one moment as the devout guardian "of a medieval superstition and fanaticism," administering the last sacrament to a dying Irishman, and at the next moment explaining the pagan origins of that sacrament in the language of the "higher criticism." He is, to adapt another description of Thomas Browne—this time Douglas Bush's—an example in the age of Darwin and Spencer of the happy marriage of science and mystical religion, contentedly and discreetly performing his function as spiritual leader for a flock of Irish who, so long as he administers their beloved sacrament properly, care nothing for his private intellectual meanderings.

Dr. Ledsmar, the scientific rationalist who amuses himself by testing Darwin's theory of hermaphroditism in plants and wonders at Ware's naïve questions about the tests, is another resident of Octavius who lives in still a different world to which Theron is a stranger—a world in which there is little emotion and only contempt for art and artists. "All art, so-called," he says to the young minister as they hear Celia Madden playing the church organ, "is decay. When a race begins to brood on the beautiful—so-called—it is a sign of rot, of getting ready to fall from the tree." Ledsmar is convinced that musicians, Celia Madden included, "stand on the very bottom rung of the ladder in the sub-cellar of human intelligence—even lower than painters and actors."

Ledsmar's respect for Father Forbes is confined to the rationalist side of the priest's divided personality; the mystical side he either ignores or explains in terms of a rationalism which is entirely too objective to appeal to Theron Ware. And since Ware's entire spiritual foundation rests on an emotional religion, the kind of thinking that Ledsmar represents is even more dangerous to the minister than is that of Father Forbes—a fact which Ware himself dimly realizes. Christian rationalism is dangerous enough to the "old, simple, primitive Methodism of Wesley and Asbury" which Ware's congregation professes; but scientific rationalism like Ledsmar's is deadly.

The third kind of unfamiliar and tempting intellectual attitude that Frederic introduces to the elm-lined streets of his upstate village of Octavius is aestheticism. Celia Madden, the talented and beautiful organist of Father Forbes's church, is not only a musician but a spokesman for the nineteenth-century gospel of beauty. Nominally a Roman Catholic like the rest of her Irish family, she is a Christian aesthete who is attracted to that side of Father Forbes's personality which Dr. Ledsmar denies. Well educated in a convent school, Celia has brought back to the village the doctrines of Ruskin and especially of Walter Pater by whose gospel she tries to live. Like Matthew Arnold, she divides people into two classes, Greeks and Jews; and she revels in being herself a Greek—

a Hellenist whose governing idea, in Arnold's phrase, is "spontaneity of consciousness." Celia, like the priest and Dr. Ledsmar, is perfectly honest with young Ware. When he comments on her "essentially religious temperament," she objects:

> "But I'm not religious at all, you know. . . . I'm as Pagan as —anything! Of course there are forms to be observed, and so on; I rather like them than otherwise. I can make them serve very well for my own system; for I am myself, you know, an out and out Greek . . . much more in sympathy with the Greek thought, the Greek theology of the beautiful and the strong, the Greek philosophy of life, and all that, than what is taught nowadays."

And later she explains:

> "I am a Catholic. . . . But I should explain that I am a Catholic only in the sense that its symbolism is pleasant to me. You remember what Schopenhauer said—you cannot have the water by itself: you may also have the jug that it is in. Very well; the Catholic religion is my jug. I put into it the things I like. They were all there thousands of years ago. The Jews threw them out; we will put them back again. We will restore art and poetry and the love of beauty, and the gentle, spiritual, soulful life."

Thus, in the quiet corner of a small upstate New York village to which he has come as an innocent and unsuspecting sectarian, Theron Ware meets currents of thought that are disturbing the very universe of his time. Unprepared and unwilling to accept them and unable to reject them in their various and appealing forms, Theron brings about his own damnation as he tries to reconcile them all to the only way of thinking he knows. As a minor character in the novel points out to him,

> "That is the greatest pity of it all. . . . You are entirely deceived about yourself. You do not at all realize how you have altered your direction, or where you are going. It was a great misfortune to you, sir, that you did not keep among your own people. . . . When you go among others . . . you have no proper understanding of what their sayings and doings really mean."

When Theron *is* finally driven back to his own kind in complete moral deterioration, he turns to the Soulsbys—half charlatans, half angels—who comfort him. But even they represent a different kind of spiritual existence from that which Theron Ware had known in the days of his innocence. They, too, are thinkers of a kind—on an entirely different level from Father Forbes, to be sure, but as effective in their way as the priest is in his. Sister Soulsby is to Ware's congregation essentially what Father Forbes is to his Irish: both provide a sincere but realistic spiritual leadership of the kind that expediency demands.

The Soulsbys, however, vivid and compelling as they are with their vaudeville techniques, represent merely a modern device brought to bear on a religious tradition that was already old in Frederic's valley. It is with the new strains of thought and the way they have infiltrated and become assimilated, if somewhat rarefied, parts of the intellectual climate of upstate New York that Frederic is really concerned in the background of *The Damnation of Theron Ware*.

Against this background, an organic part of the novel, Frederic tells his story of the young innocent who fails to recognize attacks on his simple orthodoxy (and the moral code which is part of it) when they come in subtle and alluring forms. Theron Ware is "damned" because he is unprepared by either temperament or training to recognize the thinly disguised figures of Charles Darwin and Walter Pater—to say nothing of a nineteenth-century version of Sir Thomas Browne—when he meets them either singly or in combination walking and talking along the banks of the Erie Canal.

With *The Damnation of Theron Ware*, Frederic's comprehensive examination of his region came to an end. In the four novels and the group of short stories, he had pictured his native area in every configuration that his own background and development had prepared him to discern: political, historical, socio-economic, and spiritual-intellectual. Not surprisingly, therefore, in the three years of life left to him after the writing of *Ware*, Frederic had no more to say about the region; he turned instead to an English background for his final work.

CHAPTER 6

Aristocrats and Buccaneers

I *March Hares*

FREDERIC wrote *March Hares* as an exercise for the left hand. If his notes can be trusted (and his propensity for keeping accurate dates and figures is well known to the reader), he had over thirty-five hundred words of this light romance completed by the end of August, 1895; and he finished the entire work of 47,568 words on November 19. (He could be sure that the precise figure of 47,568 words was correct; for each weekend, his daughter, Ruth, counted them, jotting the total for each manuscript page in the top corner.) Frederic, having some months earlier sent to his publishers the manuscript of his masterpiece, *The Damnation of Theron Ware,* published his new book under a pseudonym, George Forth, as he explained, because he did not want it to compete with his greater work.

Although *March Hares* gives the impression of having been written on a sudden impulse, it does not necessarily follow that Frederic composed it without having made his usual careful plans or without having thought a good deal about both plot and character. If legend carries the weight of truth, he must have had the story in mind—even if in a nebulous form—for a long time. Kate's family believes that the book was inspired by Frederic's first meeting with Kate Lyon in the British Museum; and one's imagination is not pushed too hard to make the legend credible. But that the author, like his hero in *March Hares,* met his new love on the Westminster Bridge at eight o'clock in the morning after a long night of revelry from which he had not yet sobered seems quite improbable. The notes remaining in the Frederic collection are not clear about this point. Although they are scanty and although some of the chapter outlines are missing, those left to be examined reveal the workmanlike procedure for writing typical of all Frederic fiction.

The narrative is simply structured. Vestalia Skinner (or Vestalia Peaussier as she prefers to call herself when she first meets David Mosscrop) is out of work; has been evicted by her landlady; and has, when the reader meets her, nothing more to her name than the clothes on her back and her worn-out shoes. Mosscrop, who has a kind of sinecure (a chair professing the history of the Culdees, a name which Frederic explains with the greatest plausibility imaginable), decides upon the very spot where he meets his new love to take her into his protective custody, feed and clothe her, and find a way to persuade her to marry him. The ensuing complications are ingeniously woven into the slightest of narrative outlines.

Spending an entire day with Vestalia, David takes her to his favorite restaurants, buys her new shoes and clothes, and brings her finally to the apartment of his absent friend, the Earl of Drumpipes, where she may be comfortable for the night. He is about to retire in his own apartment across the hall from Vestalia's when the Earl inconveniently returns from an extended trip to the United States. Drumpipes (better known as Archie Linkhaw, a name that he uses while traveling), who during his travels has happily lost his wife and has on board ship met a charming American girl, is thus forced to share David's apartment. Vestalia, however, escapes early the next morning, leaves no clue as to her intentions, and finds employment with the father of the American girl, Adele Skinner. Linkhaw has let Adele think that he is a commoner and that his friend Mosscrop is an earl.

Before this knot in the tale is untangled, David has found and proposed to Vestalia and has been accepted; and the Earl, or Linkhaw, has proposed to Adele and has been accepted. So the story is brought to an almost ridiculous ending when the two couples and Adele's father meet aboard Linkhaw's yacht on the Thames to celebrate the approaching marriages. To clear up the confusion in the present reader's mind, let it be said at this point that Mr. Skinner, who is connected with the Standard Oil Company, proves to be the brother of Vestalia's long dead father; thus the two girls are cousins and both seem assured of pleasant and secure lives, as much at the expense of Standard Oil as at the less than strenuous labors of their respective husbands.

The story is a sophisticated comedy of errors, of mistaken identity. It looks backward to Frederic's slight commentary on English mores in *Mrs. Albert Grundy* and it anticipates *Gloria Mundi* in its comment about the independent woman and about the improvidence of the British aristocrat. But it also displays Frederic's capacity for the light touch and for a widening range in the treatment of both subject and character. In other respects it is not a significant book. One should read it after putting one's self into Frederic's mood as it must have been at the time he wrote the fiction: a happily reminiscent mood tinted with the lighter shades of romance.

II *Gloria Mundi*

One cannot be quite sure just when Frederic began collecting material for his next novel, *Gloria Mundi.* It is possible that he had already gathered some data and made certain memoranda for it even before he finished *March Hares.* Twice in his notes for his new novel he cites from *The Nation* of January 28, 1897; but of a more indefinite nature are comments that he had drawn from "E. C.," probably Edwin Chadwick, famous British reformer and sanitary engineer, whose work Frederic might well have read, had he wished, even before going to England. In any case, besides specific pages on which he outlined his narrative structure and set down details about character and situation, Frederic used four large, double-page sheets on which he carefully wrote his own views, as well as the views of others, on such subjects as Big Estates, Business, Man at 40, Religion and Education, Art, The Sex Passion, Woman, England, The Army Set, and Children. Many of the ideas contained on these pages he expressed in *Gloria Mundi;* a few of them spilled over into *The Market-Place.* In general, these notes emphasize the differences between things as they are and things as they seem to be: they reflect, in other words, certain conclusions that Frederic had reached about contemporary English life.

Briefly, *Gloria Mundi* is the story of how Christian Tower, the son of an expatriated Englishman, learns suddenly at the age of twenty-seven that, because of the accidental deaths of those in the direct line of heirship to the title, he is to become the Duke of Glastonbury. Born and reared on the Continent, he, as the novel opens, is leaving his life as teacher and tutor to return to England at the behest of Lord Julius Torr, brother of the ancient Duke who lies dying at Caermere, the ducal seat of the Torrs. En route to England, Christian meets Frances Bailey, a London typist who runs a small establishment of professional young women engaged in secretarial work. Ultimately when he becomes the Duke, she will be his Duchess. Meantime, Christian is introduced to Caermere by Lord Julius, to his cousins (one of whom, before Christian's appearance, had expected to fall heir to the title), and to the ancient Duke himself, who lies in fumbling senility, dying, his favorite hounds stinking up his apartment to the dismay of his servants and of his doctors. Next, Christian is taken to the estate of Emanuel Torr, Lord Julius's son, where he learns of the workings of Emanuel's "System," a pseudo-social Utopia that is actually feudal in design. Then he is squired about London by a young nobleman to meet other members of England's crested and titled families. And finally, when the old Duke dies, he returns to Caermere for the funeral; and there Lord Julius tells him that all the Torr properties (which over the years Julius has saved with his wife's money) are to be restored to him unencumbered and that he is free to make his own way in life as the latest Duke of Torr. At Caermere, too, he proposes to Frances Bailey and at length persuades her to accept him.

Though laced in a web of romance, *Gloria Mundi* nevertheless presents a remarkable, penetrating contrast between appearance and reality. But it effects this contrast with such eminent good humor that one almost thinks that the author took neither himself nor his subject seriously. That, of course, was not at all the case. To Frederic's mind, shaped as it was to regard democracy as both a political and a social structure, the power and significance of the British aristocracy was an illusion. To him, some of its members were obviously the victims of self-delusion and of the dry rot of caste privilege;

some were broken financially; and others were sustained, if at all, by the importation of foreign-born and wealthy brides lured by titles.

While one can never be sure that Frederic had a particular family in mind when he created the Glastonburys for *Gloria Mundi,* one cannot question the possibility that in the idle gossip of the Savage and the National Liberal clubs in London he had heard many references to the manner in which English nobility lived and played—among these the Marlboroughs. Since on one page of his notes for the novel he mentioned the Marquess of Blandford, who was to become the ninth Duke of Marlborough, it was possible that this family served as his models, although no exact parallels can be drawn.

Not unexpectedly in a period when so much attention was paid to Utopian dreams, when the popular cry was for socialism and social reform, Frederic created in *Gloria Mundi* and then blandly debunked the medieval paradise called by its founder and director "The System." But this, too, was for Frederic an unhappy illusion. "People do not improve as world grows," he wrote elliptically in his notes for this novel. "They still fluctuate, as always did, between imitating good models, and then forgetting why they did so." Further he wrote:

> We have put the world, the mere terrestial ball, well under our feet. We have measured and photographed it. We know there no dragons in caves, no dryads in woods. The abstract no longer gets on our nerves, fancy is hamstrung. We do not brood on the mystery of life and death—the sky—the stars. . . . Roentgen Rays show us the bones in my lady's hand—that dear hand! The thought of the skull under her face could frighten Byron. Not us.[1]

Views of this nature would not make Utopian figments any more digestible to Harold Frederic than the fiction of the permanence and inviolability of an aristocratic caste which he regarded as a pump that needed constant priming. But he was no Hamlet in the graveyard; neither could he live with illusions. By training and by temperament he found the hard, real world the one to face and make the most of. Therefore, in *Gloria Mundi,* Frederic surveys through his hero's eyes both appearance and reality; and Christian Tower, who finally contemplates his future in very real terms, is guided by a happy mammalian philosophy on one hand and by the very honest, direct mind of the young woman who is to become his Duchess on the other.

Frederic finds occasion also to comment upon other aspects of English *mores*: The Fast Set, the Army, the New Woman, the "Season" in London for English nobility.[2] All of these he threads, however, into the simple pattern of his narrative; and although on occasion—as in Emanuel Torr's explication of the "System"—he overburdens *Gloria Mundi* with intrusive comment, his shrewd observation and delectable wit overlie and richly decorate this tapestry of England in its microcosmic frame.

Finally, it should be said that although well-rounded characters do emerge from this novel and although the reader finds himself responding empathically, one is led to conclude that this was, in its author's mind, a novel of ideas—not satirical in intent, but evaluative. It is without question the most English of all Frederic's works, not forgetting *March Hares.* The humor is sharper than that in *Mrs. Albert Grundy;* the romantic alliance is more serious than Mosscrop's in *March Hares.*

A closer study of *Gloria Mundi* should begin, of course, by examining Frederic's concern with the British aristocracy, for the theme about its members pervades the entire novel. First of all, Christian Tower or Torr (his father, having been forced into exile, adopted the name Tower) is something of an anomaly in the orthodoxy of the titled English class. He is plunged into a life that is strange to him: one for which he is not well fitted but one to which he must adapt himself. Fortunately for him it is Lord Julius whom he meets at the beginning, not his cousins at Caermere.

But who could say where Lord Julius might have been had he not married a wealthy Jewess from Holland? Until then he had been no more than a minor diplomatic figure with a good name, no money, and very little future. With his wife's wealth he managed to save the Torr estates; indeed he saved the ancient Duke and his family from utter ruin by wisely buying up all the mortgaged properties and allowing the Duke a low interest rate for payment. Pride of family, and little else, drove Julius to these ends; but his pride is an immense thing and his love of the image of the family is deep. Had Christian met only Lord Julius, his regard for British aristocracy would have been high. As Lady Cressage says to Christian, in speaking about Lord Julius: "He and his son are men of great intelligence and refined tastes; they would do honor to any position."

But of Christian's cousins, Lady Cressage adds: "You saw those young men this morning. They are not up to much certainly; their uncle Porlock and his sons averaged, perhaps, even a shade lower . . . but when it is all said and done, they were not so remarkably worse than other men of their class. If any of the six had succeeded to the title, he would not have been such a startling anomaly in the peerage." And this is exactly the view that Christian had of Augustine and Edward Torr when he first arrived at Caermere.

Augustine is an M. P. from his district; but, as Lady Cressage points out, he is not up to much. Edward is an army man, or has been, who would prefer to do nothing; and, were Lord Julius to settle on him a few thousand pounds a year, he would be quite satisfied to live the balance of his life hunting and riding to the hounds, drinking his rum and whisky, gambling and smoking his favorite cigars. Nor is Christian's impression of his grandfather, the Duke, much better. In a scene that would be both ghoulish and revolting had Frederic not sensed the irony of it, Christian, who meets the old man sitting half-conscious, surrounded by his dogs, reflects that

> he had expected to be overwhelmed with emotion at the meeting, but he found himself barely interested. His wandering glance chanced to take note of some of the dogs' faces about the chair. . . . He looked back again at his grandfather, and tried to say that he was a great noble, the head of an ancient and proud line, and the actual father of *his* father—but the effort failed to spur his fancy.

When Julius pushes Christian in front of the old man, explaining who he is, the Duke says merely, upon faint recognition: "Cressage could have given you five stone ten," and turns away. And when Julius asks the Duke about the hunting and whether the guns of Augustine and Edward and their friends had annoyed him, the Duke answers irrelevantly:

> "A good hearty cut across his face with a whip is what'd teach swine like Griffiths their place—and then let 'em summons you and be damned. A farmer who puts up barbed wire—no gentleman would listen to his evidence for a minute. Treat them like the vermin they are—and they'll understand that. Cressage had the proper trick with them—a kick in the stomach first and reasons afterward. That's the only way this country can be hunted."

No, Christian can hardly be impressed with his grandfather, the man whom he is to succeed. The scene is brought, for the grateful reader, to a quick ending, with Christian surmising that "there is strange blood in the Torrs." He is saved by the thought that at least Lord Julius is different from the others of the clan; and his remembrance of the kind words Julius has spoken of his own exiled, heroic father helps to check his shock and bewilderment at the behavior of the rest of the family.

Lady Cressage herself says of her dead husband and the dear heir: "He was as God made him—if the thought isn't blasphemous. He was a great, overgrown, bullying, blubbering, ignorant boy, who never got beyond the morals of the stables and kennels, and the standards of taste of the servants' hall. . . . He acted just as his rudimentary set of barbaric impulses prompted him to act."

However, it is for Christian much as Emanuel had stated the case: he could make of his position as Duke much or little or nothing at all. He could turn his responsibilities over to others as many noblemen had done and wash his hands of the "worry and labor in just that fashion." Many aristocrats, Emanuel assures him, "lead idle lives, they amuse themselves, they take all that is yielded to them and give nothing in return —and because they avoid open grossness and scandal their behavior attracts no particular attention." Everyone takes for granted that these aristocrats have done what is altogether natural. After all, they were born to a life of leisure and why should they work? With a title, the sway of power and dominion, and the deference of their inferiors and their servants, why should they try to earn the things that they own already?

Christian, disenchanted with what he has seen, seeks the image of an aristocracy that he would like to find. He fails to find it; and perhaps Frederic failed to discover it too. In fact, Christian discovers nothing better in Emanuel's "System," for it, too, is overcast with illusion. Emanuel believes that the medieval shield "was not so black as it was painted"; somehow, he thought, men had gone off the track back there in the days of Thomas More. He saw that

> mankind then and there had come close to the possibilities of a golden age. True, it had wandered off miserably again, into all manner of blind lanes and morasses, until it floundered now in a veritable Dismal Swamp of individualism, menaced on the one side by the millionaire slave-hunter, on the other by the spectral anarchist, and still the fools in its ranks cried out ceaselessly for further progress.

In his "System" Emanuel has found all the answers: the panacea for all diseases of modern society. His is a cooperative pattern, medieval in spirit and in form, that perpetuates the caste structure in the social organism. But Christian, as he listens to Emanuel's explication of the system and reflects upon it at length, grows more and more skeptical as the days pass. He is happy at last to discover that Frances Bailey has little more than contempt for the plan. She says to him:

> "What you see in him [Emanuel] is a triumph of the Semitic passion for working a problem out to its ultimate conclusion. When you consider it, what has he done? Merely discovered, by tremendous labor and energy, the smoothest possible working arrangement of the social system which his class regards as the best for itself, and hence for all mankind—the system which exalts a chosen few, and keeps all the rest in subjection. My dear sir, things do not rise higher than their source."

Thereupon she castigates the Torrs—in essence the whole aristocratic class—saying that they came by their estates only by stealing the birthright of thousands of innocent human beings whom they have abused as beasts. They put these unfortunates into irons and drove them like so much cattle.

And as for Emanuel's forebears, even Lord Julius's beloved wife—Frances Bailey flares out at them: They had made their money "by the most frightful and blood-stained human slavery in the poisonous jungles of the Dutch East Indies—that, and an ancient family business of international usury, every dirty penny in which if you followed it far enough, meant the flaying alive of a peasant, or the starvation of his little children." These, she says, are the things that Emanuel has inherited; and, although he is admittedly ashamed of them, he would not repudiate them. In fine, his "System" is no better than its master; and if it is his wish to be a gentle man, seeking only the happiness of those around him, he also still maintains himself well and has his servants to tend his wants. Driven by the very passion of which Frances Bailey speaks, Emanuel finally breaks in health and is forced to give up all that he has lived for. The reader is aware that without his leadership the "System" will swiftly fall into decline.

Faced with two unacceptable choices, Christian must nevertheless come to some conclusions, must make some decisions. He will eschew all thought of superimposing upon modern society an outmoded monstrosity from the Middle Ages; for he agrees with Frances Bailey that Emanuel has deluded himself and has, in short, formalized and perpetuated a social structure that would impede rather than advance man in his struggle to exist.

In this respect, of course, Christian is thinking and speaking for Frederic himself. Emanuel's "Dismal Swamp of individualism" was for the author not quite so dismal as Emanuel would have it. Frederic's notes, under the caption "People," reveal something of his attitude:

> Individuals in a crowd—at theater or great dinner table—each still alone, pursuing own little plans, desires, conscious of vast accumulated personal history no other will ever, can ever, know.[3]

And for Frederic to accept a social pattern that would deny the right of the individual, that would place him inescapably in one mold or another was unthinkable. Christian's disillusionment with the "System" was also Frederic's. At the same time, if Frederic had once been attracted to the Utopian dreams of

Morris and Ruskin, or to those of Bellamy and Howells, he now rejects them totally.

Whatever Frederic's private views, Christian becomes the Duke of Glastonbury and compromises himself by submitting to the form, at least, of the aristocratic title and all that it seems to imply. However, Frederic allows himself—and Christian—an escape route. In his notes for the novel, he wrote:

> Custom is the ultimate law—Mq Blandford was Radical, but as Duke he fell into groove. This weight of habitude is most powerful thing man has to encounter.
>
> Yes—but here Duke had been gross failure, even from Duke's standpoint [this is Glastonbury, of course].
>
> Fresh ground is offered to Christian—he can be what he likes, with restored estates, etc.[4]

Whether the Marquess of Blandford was indeed a radical, as Frederic appears to have believed, is not important here; that he fell into the groove, allowing himself to be overcome by the weight of habitude, that he failed from his standpoint to achieve some particular—even radical—objective, just as Emanuel failed, *is* important. But Christian may make his own choice, though he cannot always do as he pleases.

What he plans, he tells Frances Bailey following the funeral of his grandfather:

> "I think that if a man is honest and ambitious for good things, and has some brains, he can grow to be equal to any task that will be laid on him. A man is only a man after all. He did not make this world, and he cannot do with it what he likes. . . . We learn only one thing from all the numberless millions who have gone before us—that man is less important than he thinks he is. I have a high position thrust upon me. *Eh bien*! I am not going to command the sun to stand still. I am not going to believe that I ought to revolutionize human society before I die. There will be many men after me. If one or two of them says of me that I worked hard to do well, and that I left things a trifle better than I found them, then what more can I desire?"

Christian will, then, accept the responsibility of the Dukedom; but the illusion of the titled aristocrat he will not accept, nor will he accept life as Edward and Augustine Torr would have it. They, at least, will have to become useful even in their limited ways. He will marry a commoner and be of some service to his society. What more could be asked of him? For after all, the time will come for him, as for all men, when the world has nothing more to offer than "a little hole . . . for him to be buried in and forgotten. . . ." This is the pattern of reality. *Sic transit gloria mundi.*

In many respects, this novel must have been for Frederic a kind of summing up. Like Christian, he had come to England from another continent, eager with expectation, full of hopes yet to be realized, ambitious to fulfill his destiny in the world. And the world at moment of his arrival in London presented limitless possibilities. By 1898, if Christian speaks for him, he he believed that

> . . . he was as much alone in London . . . as he had been when he first set foot in it. Indeed, was he not the poorer today by all those lost illusions and joyous, ardent hopes now faded to nothingness?

Obviously Frederic used his characters as mouthpieces. His views on the "New Woman," the professional class of young women that had come into being, for example, he summarized in his notes. Most of these he used in *Gloria Mundi*—some of them almost verbatim, as was his practice—in his portrait of Frances Bailey as a member of that group. He described them as

> Hens who won't sit. . . . The new professional class, which earns its own living and has come through the mill of responsibility, and will not accept the old nonsense invented for and imposed upon parasites.
>
> Some younger women are now asking questions or rather proceeding on theory they answered them. The woful trouble is that the reading furnished them . . . is crammed with senseless falsehoods, gaps. Literally no truth is told them at all. This is by far the gravest disadvantage they labor under.
>
> For example, when recent boom of hysterical fiction on, great clamor made about truth being revealed to women, of women, by women, at last. But it wasn't truth after all. They get truth neither from critics, flattering friends nor their authors.

False, conventional ideals, manners, values, presented to them all sides. It only the professional woman, working for herself, who begun to find this out.[5]

But the point of the illustration is not just that Frederic was preparing to write a novel. He was doing his thinking on paper and much of what he thought, in this case certainly, he utilized. The notes disclose the extent to which *Gloria Mundi* is a kind of intellectual autobiography; and though the novel may fail in other respects to measure up to *Ware, In the Valley,* or even to *The Market-Place,* it can be read as a revelation not only of Frederic's attitudes toward the England in which he lived and worked but also of his conclusions about a design for living. The pity is that not all of his notations—the brilliant comment, the penetrating observations that cut to the core of things—made their way into this or any other fiction that he created. As it turned out, he had only one more novel to write before he was to be struck down by illness from which he never recovered.

III *The Market-Place*

In *Gloria Mundi,* Christian Torr declared to Frances Bailey: "A man is only a man after all. He did not make this world, and he cannot do with it what he likes. . . . We learn only one thing from all the numberless millions who have gone before us—that man is less important than he thinks he is." And if one seeks to draw a meaningful conclusion from Frederic's last novel, *The Market-Place,* Christian's expression of this mature and humane viewpoint would probably serve better than any other. For in many respects *The Market-Place* continues for Frederic to be a summing up; it is as if he knew the time had come for him to put down his pen forever. Frederic rejected in his world all such men as the buccaneer hero of his tale, Joel Thorpe, just as he had already rejected the Edward and Augustine Torrs and the whole aristocratic concept of ducal authority in *Gloria Mundi.*

The Market-Place was published posthumously, first as a serial in *The Saturday Evening Post,* where it appeared on December 17, 1898, nearly two months after the author died, and ran through the issue of June 3, 1899. Then it was printed simultaneously by Frederick A. Stokes in New York and by Heinemann in London. At first glance, it may seem to the modern reader to have been first-rate fiction for the *Post,* exploiting as it does the success of the rugged individualist on the one hand while suggesting, on the other, that its hero has a democratic urge to help the down-trodden. But to the discriminating reader it is a complex piece of writing in whose subtle insinuations one hears the sharp rebuke of satire and the slightly derisive laughter of irony.

Celia Madden, whom readers first saw in *The Damnation of Theron Ware* and who reappears here, says of the hero at the story's end: "I shall always insist . . . that crime was his true vocation." His sister, reflecting upon his machinations, thinks to herself: "All his voyages and adventures and painful enterprises had been informed by the desire of the buccaneer—the passion to reap where others had sown, or, at the worst, to get something for nothing." And Joel Stormont Thorpe, English-born son of a London bookseller, is in fact a buccaneer: immoral in his operations; arrogant; domineering; and, like the genus of which he is typical, totally self-interested but capable of moments of tenderness when the mood for it is upon him. He is a thoroughly disagreeable man around whom Frederic skillfully contrives to draw a set of scoundrels and and with whom he associates romantically a beautiful but weak woman who is attracted by his wealth—and by his virility. Yet, astoundingly enough, the author makes the tale logical and altogether plausible; for its hero at times is not completely reprehensible.

A runaway from his bookselling family, Thorpe has, when the story opens, returned to England after a fifteen-year absence. He set out to make his fortune; and, failing time and again in exploits that carried him to China, the Dutch Indies, Australia, the Argentine—in short, all over the world—he at last bought a rubber plantation and brought back to London a few thousand pounds with which he plans to exploit his purchase on the market-place. With the assistance of a shrewd Scot, Colin Semple, he manipulates a "corner" on bogus stock in rubber consols; forces, with nothing more than bluff, the hands of old-time operators; and does in fact come off with a comfortable fortune. Meanwhile, he has put his nephew and niece through school, has consorted with aristocrats, and has won the hand of Lady Edith Cressage.

At the end of this fast-moving story, Thorpe is seeking some way to increase and expand his power. He discovers that under the guise of helping the underdog, he can usefully put his cash to work to lift himself into a position of supreme influence. He expects ultimately to land in Parliament. "London has been waiting for an organizer—a leader—for a hundred years," he says. "The right kind of man, going the right way to work can stand London on its head, as surely as I can burn this cigar. And I'm going to have a try at it." Thus, at the end of the tale Thorpe is precisely the same man he was at the beginning: utterly ruthless and wholly without conscience, he refuses to let anyone or anything stand in his way once he has set his course of action.

The Market-Place looks backward to two other Frederic novels: *The Damnation of Theron Ware* and *Gloria Mundi*. Celia Madden reappears from *Ware* far less the Greek than she had been and as a creature of considerably greater modesty and humility. In fact, she makes what one might call her *apologia;* for, midway in the narrative, she summarizes for Thorpe her analysis of his character—and a shrewd one it is:

> "I should say that you possessed a capacity for sudden and capricious action in large matters, equally impatient of reasoning and indifferent to consequences, which might be very awkward, and even tragic, to people who happened to annoy you, or stand in your road. You have the kind of organization in which within a second, without any warning or reason, a passing whim may have worked itself up into an imperative law—something you must obey."

Having served as Frederic's mouthpiece for this speech, she also explains how damaging the kind of power Thorpe possesses may be to others. Thorpe's organization, she confesses, is her own—or *was.* In her teens she had her own money and her own power of a limited sort. "But I know what I did with my power," she continues. "I spread trouble and misery about me. . . ." Following the death of her father and brother and other sobering events, she discovered, however, that she was still young enough to "stop short and take stock" of herself and to say that there were certain roads that she planned never again to set foot on. Those who have read *Ware* recall readily her evening with Theron when she played Chopin for him and accomplished a kind of vicarious seduction of the poor man. After Theron's departure, she poured herself a bit of Benedictine in the glass that Theron had used; smiling to herself and musing: "The smile warmed itself suddenly into a joyous laugh. She tossed the glass aside, and, holding out her flowing skirts with both hands, executed a swinging pirouette in front of the gravely beautiful statue of the armless woman." At the time, of course, she knew well the extent of her conquest; but she was indifferent to the consequences of her shameless flirtation. Her confession is, therefore, something of a revelation.

In re-introducing characters from former novels, Frederic did what many another writer has done. But he uses these characters in *The Market-Place* not only to attract readers who knew them in the other novels but also to serve the useful purposes of effecting contrast in characterization and of underscoring and emphasizing certain ideas that he wishes to set forth. Celia Madden, for example, is one to whom a reader gives his earnest attention; for she is one of the most intriguing and most disturbing women Frederic created. She did not, as Frank Harris once asserted, run away with *The Damnation*. As we have earlier seen, Frederic clearly made her a complex of gracious lady, hoyden, artist, temptress, and woman of the world. He regarded her as WOMAN: inexplicable in her actions and even contradictory; but we understand by her confession in the later novel that she was in *Ware* a portrait of Eve. In *The Market-Place* she has altered and matured, just as Frederic himself had; and it is also clear that he prefers the older Celia Madden.

Lady Cressage and Christian Tower, or Torr (now the Duke of Glastonbury), likewise reappear from *Gloria Mundi* as characters in this book. Edith Cressage—her title came through her first disastrous marriage—is the passive woman in *The Market-Place*. She seems not to know what she wants in life and admits this fact to Celia, her confidante in the matter of her relationship with Thorpe. Only once does Lady Cressage come close to asserting herself. When the two women are carrying on an extended discussion of Thorpe, Celia, commenting upon the enigmatic coldness in Thorpe's eyes, says that in the dull glaze coming over them from time to time, one "can see a hundred thousand dead men." Lady Cressage replies defensively, "But may that not be merely the visible sign of an exceptionally strong and masterful character?" She is, in fact, almost hypnotized by Thorpe's masterfulness; she is won to him not only because he has the money that she lacks and resents not having but also because she is fascinated by the very characteristics in him that are void in her: definiteness of action, self-assertiveness, the power to move men and to control them. Fundamentally, of course, for her the attraction is of the weak for the strong.

Christian Torr reappears only briefly with his lady, the Duchess of Glastonbury, the Frances Bailey of *Gloria Mundi*. But he serves Frederic's purpose of marking the shift in modern English life, a transition as tumultuous and significant in Frederic's eyes as that which occurred in the 14th century when, following the devastating plague, a new yeoman class arose. England was man-hungry then: the feudal pattern was broken and the bourgeois man come to birth. The Duke speaks thus for the author:

> "The nobleman, the prince, was a great person in the times when he monopolized wealth. . . . He had the arts and the books and the musicians and the silks and velvets, and the bath-tubs—everything that made existence gorgeous—all to himself. He had wars to amuse himself with, and the seven deadly sins. . . . The barriers are down now. Everything which used to be exclusively the nobleman's is now within everybody's reach, including the sins. . . . As an institution, he descends from a period when the only imaginable use for wealth was to be magnificent with it. But now in this business age, where the recognized use of wealth is to make more wealth, he is so much out of place that he has even forgotten how to be magnificent."

The Duke can of course speak knowingly. For he had witnessed in the earlier novel the failure of his cousin's experiment in modern feudalism and the folly of imagining that an outmoded medieval structure could be superimposed upon a long-established *laissez-faire* system. Emanuel Torr's plan was not William Morris's cooperative venture by any means. And Frederic saw plainly the reasons for the Torr system. He saw, too, the cracking up of the old aristocracy and the rise of the power-man. In *The Market-Place* Lord Plowden would collapse but for the munificence of such men as Thorpe—if indeed men of Thorpe's stamp chose to be munificent at all—just as Eddy and Gus Torr would have collapsed but for Christian's munificence. Men of this mold, Frederic understood, were not born to compete in the modern world; they soon would die out unless they could adapt and struggle to lift themselves out of the morass of a hopeless tradition.

Today, as one witnesses the workings of the National Trust, with the ancient ducal manor houses open to the public for a half crown—on display one or more days each week so that the noble owners can meet the costs of maintenance—one sees how acute Frederic's perception actually was. The men who had helped build the British Empire were a dying race even as the Empire reached its zenith in 1888 when the good Queen Victoria was crowned Empress of India and added to her long list of royal titles. Mr. Churchill had no wish as prime minister, he said, to preside over the disintegration of His Majesty's Empire; but preside over it he did, nonetheless; and in this respect Frederic's analysis was almost prophetic.

It is not the plight of the aristocracy, however, but Joel Stormont Thorpe who absorbs the reader—and his canny sister, Louisa, who possesses all the scruples, all the integrity, and all the quiet acceptance of life that her ruthless brother lacks. Since Frederic focuses his attack and his implacable satire upon Thorpe, every other character, even Louisa, fades into the backdrop of the narrative. He is in fact the closest approach that Frederic ever made to a Nietzschean figure, and *The Market-Place* the closest he came to utilizing a deterministic philosophy.

That Frederic studied Nietzsche seems very likely. Even the title of his novel, *The Market-Place,* can scarcely be regarded as a coincidence. For in *Thus Spake Zarathustra,* Nietzsche wrote: "When I went among men for the first time, I committed the anchorite's folly, the great folly: I stood in the market-place." Both *Beyond Good and Evil* and *Thus Spake Zarathustra* were known in England in the nineties, and there can be little doubt that Frederic made his acquaintance with at least the more generally known and understood of Nietzschean concepts.[1]

One cannot but note how closely Thorpe is identified with Nietzsche's concept of the will to power. Following Celia Madden's clever analysis of his character, Thorpe replies insistently: "There's nothing else in the world so big as power—strength. If you have that you can get everything else." He likes the sense of power exemplified in the fine furniture of his office; the feeling that he can manipulate his Board; the sentient awareness of being in a position where he can give or take away, as he does with Plowden and Semple and the elder Fromentin—men with whom he is directly or indirectly associated in his operations on the stock exchange. He also finds pleasure in helping his nephew and niece, in looking forward to the purchase of his own manor house and gardens and stables, and in having the proper lackeys to serve him; but his pleasure is derivative: he can do and buy because he has the power given him by his newly acquired wealth.[2] He never enjoys his power quite so much as when he can squeeze two men of his own type and utilize the unscrupulous methods by which these men themselves have come into positions of wealth and power. In one sense he finds pleasure in the power he has over Lady Cressage—even if he has a moment or two of trepidation about acquiring her as his wife.

Moreover, he is almost without conscience; and Nietzsche simply rejected the whole apparatus of conscience. Thorpe gives way for a time to certain fears of exposure by two men who had been in Mexico when he purchased the rubber plantation for which he later created his bogus stock. But he sends one of them off with Lady Cressage's father to drink himself to death; the other he at last dismisses as, after all, inconsequential.

Nietzsche's idea, then, that the will to power is more nearly fundamental than the will to live is to Joel Thorpe wholly acceptable;[3] and he is not merely looking for security or for a preservation of self.[4] He seeks ever-increasing power to be able to master and transmute not only his own condition but also the very environment in which he lives. He is not the victim of a sense of guilt; for he rejects the weakness of such men as Lord Plowden, even if at first he envies the nobleman. He merely mounts Plowden's broad shoulders to ride him into a position from which he can use the young lord to acquire a knowledge of how a nobleman lives and conducts himself among his peers.

But Thorpe uses Plowden in much the same way he uses nearly everyone with whom he comes into contact. He acts as if he were following precisely Nietzsche's view that a man "who strives for great things regards everyone whom he meets on his way as either a means or a delay or an obstacle."[5] Yet he turns on Plowden, whom he has helped but who has not the skill or the will to use cleverly the advantage against Thorpe that he has. By exploiting one man, Plowden might easily have blocked Thorpe's attempt to gain a "corner" on rubber consols; but, as he does not possess the instinct for power that Thorpe has, he fails altogether in his move to blackmail him. Scornful of the younger man's weakness, Thorpe, however, allows himself to be condescendingly magnanimous.

Having won his wealth, his wife, and his estates, Thorpe finds himself less satisfied than he might be. He can eat and drink somewhat more and better than the poor man, buy more clothes and shoes, and take life easier. But he finds a limit to his enjoyment of the power he has achieved and the position he has reached. He has a need, therefore, to expand and increase his power in some way. In true Nietzschean fashion and in his inexplicable twist of reason, he decides upon a way in which he can become a superman.[6]

Frederic's last thrust of satire is one of the most skilfully conceived passages in any of his novels. An innocent reader might easily gloss over the piquant irony of Thorpe's great play by which he announces gravely to Lady Cressage that he will "rule England." One must re-read this passage almost in its entirety to be aware of its innuendoes; but a small portion will suggest Thorpe's obsession with power:

> Considering that he had but dimly drifted about heretofore on the outskirts of the altruistic impulse, it was surprisingly plain to him now that he intended to be a philanthropist. . . . His old dormant, formless lust for power stirred again in his pulses. What other phase of power carried with it such re-

wards, such gratitudes, such humble subservience on all sides as far as the eye could reach. . . .

What could not a man of real breadth and energy and force of character, do in London with two hundred thousand pounds? Why, he could make himself master of the town! . . . He could reverse the partisan complexion of the Metropolitan delegation, and lead to Westminster a party of his own, a solid phalanx of disciplined men, standing for the implacable Democracy of reawakened London. With such a backing, he could coerce ministries at will, and remake the politics of England. The *role* of Great Oliver himself was not too hopelessly beyond the scope of such a vision.

In this manner, changes could and would be made; and he, Thorpe, would be the prime mover. In his impatience and restlessness, Thorpe is as much aware of the inevitability and necessity of flux as he is of the strength of his will to power. The plan that he conceives exhilarates him. When his wife sees him, shortly after his reverie, she sees in his face "the visage of a conquerer—of a man gathering within himself, to expend upon his fellows, the appetites, energies, insensibilities, audacities of a beast of prey." One might think that Frederic had taken the passage or a good part of it immediately from Nietzsche.[7] In fact there need be little more to assure the reader that Frederic was versed in Nietzschean philosophy.

But still other Nietzschean concepts are reflected in the pages of *The Market-Place*. One has, for example, no sense of the pastoral in the environment of Thorpe's estate, nor of a shepherd of the local flock saying masses in the chapel on Sundays. With religion Thorpe has nothing to do. With Nietzsche, he has rejected the slave morality of a Christian world.

Joel Stormont Thorpe is a villain extraordinary! No other Frederic character, save Theron Ware, is quite so relentlessly subjected to his author's scorn; yet Frederic remains totally outside the fiction, or almost so, as he views and condemns with pitiless satire the criminal record not only of the Thorpe type depicted but also of the society that permits him to flourish. In the broader sense, Frederic rejected the whole canon of Nietzschean philosophy as he understood it. If he was wrong in his interpretation, he was probably not the first and surely not the last to misconceive it.

Thorpe's sister, Louisa, is by contrast, a delight to the reader. She has never believed her brother, nor believed in him; and no one knows her reaction better than Thorpe. Indeed he reminds her that she "never did believe in me, as a sister should" at the very moment that she is introduced in the narrative. For her children's sake she accepts his help with their education and travel; but she will not live in a home that he is willing to buy for her, nor will she abandon the shop in which she has been reared and in which her father and her grandfather had made their living. She prefers to make her threepence profit by selling a book at one and six than to own the Bank of England—if owning it calls for dishonest practices. As she regards a check that he has left so that she may prepare her children for a trip to the continent with their uncle, "the implacable legend" runs for her: "Even now I don't believe in him."

When Thorpe explains to her the manner in which he is manipulating the stock market and forcing a number of his competitors almost to the wall, she says, meditating the whole sequence of activity calmly: "It's cruel, isn't it?"

Lightly, Thorpe replies: "Everything in the City is cruel . . . All speculative business is cruel."

Cruel, too, is the manner in which Thorpe leads her children, Alfred and Julia, away from her, spoils them with his money, and makes them almost ashamed of their mother. His thoughtlessness she bears with dignity although at times her heart is sorely embittered by her loss. Her integrity and her independence remain unshaken. She will live her life in accord with her own principles, and these are not by any means her brother's principles. Louisa is a character of whom George Gissing might have made much—or later, Arnold Bennett. Wisely, Frederic did not allow her to play too great a part; for though she could have been the perfect counterpoint to her brother's heavy burden, Frederic remained, by keeping her properly submerged, the composer in control of his score. Thorpe is not for a moment lost to the reader. He will, one is convinced, end by standing London on its head. Crime is, indeed, his true vocation. But at last, as Christian Torr would say, what will he have gained beyond "a little hole . . . for him to be buried in and forgotten"? Such is Frederic's question.

CHAPTER 7

Summation: Marks of Greatness

THE YEARS of Frederic's lifetime witnessed in both England and the United States what has been called the triumphant rise of realism as a literary mode. Realism had, of course, prevailed since the first quarter of the century in such countries as France, for example; but it was slower to make headway in England where a literary taste had not yet developed for books dealing with the harsher facts of life, or in America where a complex of frontier humor and romance only grudgingly made way for a franker analysis of the American scene and character. Whatever gave it impetus—the rise of the scientific inquiry with its emphasis upon laboratory methods, the growing urbanization of life and a consequent focalizing of attention upon the multiplex problems of the human situation, a revolt against sentimentality and saccharine romanticism—the lands in which Harold Frederic was to live found more and more of their creative artists adopting as a primary rule of writing what William Dean Howells called "the truthful treatment of material."

But realism was not accepted universally or without protest; in fact, both the critic and the reading public complained against it. Thomas Hardy's *Under the Greenwood Tree* (1872) and *A Pair of Blue Eyes* (1873) found quick favor with an English audience, for they contained enough of the innocuously romantic as not to offend. But Hardy was forced to add the romantic affair of Thomasin Yeobright and Diggory Venn to his *Return of the Native,* one of his greatest novels, before it was acceptable for serialization. Likewise he found himself compelled seriously to expurgate *Tess of the d'Urbervilles* for magazine publication, but when the novel was restored to its entirety later, it was attacked and denounced. Although the restraints of a Victorian society were less severe in 1891 when *Tess* first appeared than they had been even ten years earlier, they were so rigorous that when Hardy brought out *Jude the Obscure* in 1895, he found himself abused roundly and he abandoned novel writing altogether.

In the United States, as early as 1883, Charles Dudley Warner regarded realistic fiction as that which presented "a wholly unidealized view of human society."[1] He attacked it because, as he said, it considered only the worst phases of American society, employing the extreme in analysis of character and substituting psychological study for action. In fact, he found little if anything in realism to recommend it to writers or readers. When one examines the records of the 1890's, one finds that the lists of bestsellers (excepting a few works by well-established authors) rarely contained titles of realistic novels.

Nevertheless, the interest in realism as a literary technique somehow persisted. As a nineteenth-century journalist, Harold Frederic might surely have been expected to respond in his own writing to the current impulses. And so he did. *Seth's Brother's Wife, The Lawton Girl, The Damnation of Theron Ware, The Copperhead, Marsena,* and other of his Civil War stories, mark him as essentially a realist. He admitted in his preface to the Uniform Edition of *In the Sixties* that he had been influenced by the writings of the French historical novelists, Erckmann-Chatrian, for the treatment he ultimately gave his materials in the war fictions. Yet he also confessed, in 1885, that when he began his writing of *Seth* he did not know "how to make a book of any kind, let alone a historical book of the kind which should be the most difficult and exacting of all."[2] In other words, at the very outset of his literary career Frederic had no clearly defined theory about artistic creation. He was impelled to write; because he had been thoroughly disciplined in newspaper offices as both reporter and editor, he was prepared to write well; he believed that the writing of fiction would give him money and a much wished-for independence from newspaper deadlines.

Curiously enough, on the title page of one manuscript that he left unfinished, Frederic once scribbled the names of four

Hardy novels: "Madding Crowd, Trumpet Major, Blue Eyes, Mayor Casterbridge."[3] Apparently he made these notations at some time in the early 1890's; but, whatever the case, all these Hardy fictions had been published by 1886 and of them certainly *Far from the Madding Crowd* and *The Mayor of Casterbridge* can be called realistic. Frederic must have been familiar with them and he may have been influenced by them.

How much of other English writers of his own time he had read one cannot now be certain. Probably he had read a good deal not only of the English but also of the continental fiction. Even in his Bedford Square home (1887-1892) works by Dostoevski, Tolstoy, Gorky, Bourget, de Maupassant, Balzac, as well as by Hardy, Meredith, and Dickens and many other English authors, appeared on his study shelves. His daughter wrote: "The only book that my father ever took way from me was 'The Book of Martyrs,' by one Fox—it was full of the most gruesome details and pictures, and I *loved* it!"[4] From this statement one can see that Frederic's interest was not in the contemporary only.

Among contemporary writers, Frederic recognized William Dean Howells as a "master" of fiction. In 1888 he met and talked with Howells. Although this was their only meeting, Frederic wrote the "master" in 1890, just before sailing for England, expressing his regret that he could not again be in Boston to talk with the chief exponent of American realism. "I do not like to go without saying to you," he wrote, "that I shall carry away to London no other recollection of my visit equal in value to the memory of my call upon you. I am richer for having come to know you—and the stronger for having gained a closer insight into your beliefs and feelings. It by no means follows that I see all things as you do, or that the work I am going to do will wholly please you, but I am sure both the vision and the performance will be helped by the fact of my knowing you."[5]

In this and in two other letters, Frederic expressed his highest regard for Howells. But, then, he almost invariably wrote with enthusiasm, infusing his letters with his irrepressible warmth of nature; he wrote, in fact, just as he talked: earnestly and forcefully. He was not insincere. At the moment he wrote, probably no man could have been more sincere.

Nevertheless, occasionally some exaggeration of sentiment appears in Frederic's letters—enough, at any rate, to warrant a discounting of statements that have been made regarding Howells' influence upon him.

Undoubtedly Frederic's work as a journalist did much to shape his style. From his earliest days as a reporter and then as editor of the Utica *Observer,* he had learned to deal with facts, to examine life, and to reveal it as he found it. But his interests were too broad and his creative efforts too varied in treatment to place him unequivocally in the ranks of the realists. *In the Valley* is plainly a historical romance. *The Return of the O'Mahony* is a first-rate comedy. *March Hares* is pure fantasy, light, gay, decidedly whimsical. *Gloria Mundi* is too much a commentary upon English life and manners, fringed about with the gauzy stuff of romance, to warrant placing it in the category of realistic novels. *The Market-Place,* for all its realistic approach to the crudities of the business world, is, as we have seen, a not-too-thinly veiled satire.

One can scarcely dismiss a packet of short stories in which Frederic dealt with the Ireland or England of long ago. "The Path of Murtogh," "How Dickon Came by his Name," and "Where Avon into Severn Flows" are typical romances. Moreover, as one examines the numerous incomplete manuscripts now to be read in the Library of Congress collection, one finds that occasionally Frederic roamed even more widely. He began, for example, a semi-poetic drama with a background of Anglo-Saxon England. He completed another drama (untitled and unproduced) dealing with mesmerism—or, as it seems in certain parts of the play, self-hypnosis. He left uncompleted a dozen other dramatic pieces and short stories, many of which could hardly be classified as realistic fiction.

Although it is true that Frederic was an indefatigable searcher after the facts that would give substance to his creative efforts and that he did not like to plunge into a story or a play without adequate preparation, his conscientiousness was as much a part of his background and training in journalism as a reflection of his interest in realism as an artistic mode. Examining closely all the known extant notes, letters, and manuscripts (except those in the missing Keen Papers), one finds scarcely a line devoted to literary theory.

But Frederic unquestionably talked about the subject. His meeting with William Dean Howells, his membership in the Ghouls Club in London, his evenings at the Savage and the National Liberal clubs, his friendship with many well-known writers of his day—all these associations gave him opportunity to discuss artistic principles at length. Probably it was in just such company as he found at the Ghouls that he had occasion to talk about literature. Sir Alfred Watson, son of Frederic's good friend, Aaron Watson, has said that his father, Spencer Leigh Hughes, A. E. Fletcher, Bart Kennedy, and Harold Frederic made up one of the most congenial and stimulating groups ever found at the National Liberal; and, meeting often in the evenings, these men, newspapermen and writers, discussed literature as much as they argued over politics and international problems.[6] With his great propensity for conversation, Frederic had many opportunities to introduce the subject of literature and literary techniques; and, although he often took the lead in a discussion, he probably absorbed much of what he heard and formulated some guide lines for his own creative activity.

In any case, he wrote a prodigious amount of fiction and nonfiction and he was read (even if not popularly) by a large group of discriminating people who understood and appreciated his efforts. Yet it would be something of an oversimplification to fit him snugly into a school of realists and fail to recognize those other aspects of his career and of his multifaceted personality that formed Harold Frederic, the artist. Had he lived a longer life, had he been free from the deadlines of his paper, and had he been less driven by the needs of two households, the patterns of his literary output might have become more clearly defined. Nevertheless, it must be admitted that many of his major works are strongly realistic, no matter what the impulses from which they derived, and that they push out of the drawingroom realism of Howells and James to deal with the more moving and vital forces at work in a less polite and sequestered world of men and women. Not the Back Bay in Boston nor the tea tables of England and the Continent, but the hardier farm and town along the Mohawk became the milieu for Frederic's best-known fictions.

I *Frederic and His British Contemporaries*

In order properly to assess Frederic's achievement and to place him in relationship to the writers of his day, one must first examine, in review, the brief span of his life as a writer and sift through the critical opinions of his contemporaries, both English and American. As has already been pointed out, for the last fourteen years of his life he lived in London and in Kenley, in the Coulsdon parish in Surrey, just fifteen miles south of London. These years mark the most productive period of his career. For besides sending to the New York *Times* weekly dispatches which he assiduously prepared and cabled to his home office, he yet drove himself to write novels, short stories, and numerous articles for English newspapers and magazines.

Harold Frederic's reputation as a writer was more secure in England than it was in America. In general, English critics and reviewers seem to have been kinder to him than his fellow countrymen, and certainly not because they were any less perceptive than their American counterparts. It should be remembered that Frederic had to meet readers already accustomed to the best work of Thomas Hardy, of George Gissing, of Meredith and Butler and Mrs. Humphrey Ward, of G. B. Shaw, and the younger crowd of writers including such diverse personalities as H. G. Wells and Rider Haggard. One must recall, of course, that even as early as 1887, he had become a figure to contend with among British journalists and clubmen. As an associate of the New York *Times,* he had something of a ready-made reputation that he enhanced by astute reporting and more than usual analytical acumen. This fact alone drew attention to the robust young American, but it cannot suffice as an explanation for the praise that he received from British critics. The obvious fact is that English critics and reviewers read his work and valued it.

He was not by any means at once or universally accepted as a front-ranking author. Some of his early work such as *The Lawton Girl* drew scant commendation. A reviewer found this novel not unlike other American novels of the time in "its taste for detail amounting to talent, a cultivated style not quite easy enough, a delay in coming to the point of the story, and an unfortunate want of consideration for the reader's patience."[7] The book was creditably written, this reviewer went on to say, but lacked both vigor and originality.

By the time that *The Copperhead* had reached the public, however, Frederic's stature had increased. In fact, one critic stated that Frederic's performance in his Civil War stories was altogether satisfactory; to him, each story contained a significant promise of better things to come from the American's pen.[8] In this connection it is interesting to note that in his Frederic article published in the *Chap-Book* for March 15, 1898, Stephen Crane bemoaned the fact that an earlier edition of *The Copperhead* sold fewer than a thousand copies in America; and he berated American critics who had so ignored Frederic's unswerving skill as a craftsman. In the main, though, Frederic was to get the greatest encouragement from his English contemporaries.

When *The Damnation of Theron Ware* reached readers with its English title, *Illumination*, Frederic had won not a little prestige as a novelist and writer of short stories. *Illumination* came close to making him famous. S. L. Gwynn, writing for the *Edinburgh Review* and commenting upon the work of several authors, including Gertrude Atherton, Mary Wilkins [Freeman], Stephen Crane, and Richard Harding Davis, considered *Illumination* a great novel—as probably the strongest and most fully representative to have come from an American writer in many years. "It is not to be expected," Gwynn wrote, "that the novel of pure analysis would go on for ever being the drawing-room production to which Mr. Howells accustomed us. Men and women naturally demanded some stronger meat than his elaboration of fine-spun quarrels over a look or an intonation. The American novel has eschewed romance and incident, and, to excite or even to interest continuously, it must take the study of those emotions which move man and woman most profoundly."[9]

Mr. Gwynn did not stand alone in his praise of Frederic's work. A strong chorus of voices lauding the American could be heard in 1896. Carrying the burden, *The Spectator* likened Frederic's *Illumination* to *The Scarlet Letter* in its artistic touch, calling it the best novel that he had produced and saying that it placed him nearly at the head of the newest school of American fiction.[10] *The Daily Chronicle* joined in harmoniously: "Mr. Frederic is winning his way by sure steps to the foremost ranks of writers of fiction. . . ."[11] *The Westminster Gazette* and *The Manchester Guardian* echoed in counterpoint to the *Chronicle* by affirming that Frederic had gained a front rank among living novelists and that *Illumination* was a rarity: a book of genuine importance. Even the great Gladstone thought it to be a masterpiece of character drawing.[12]

Though Frank Harris, the *Saturday Review* editor, thought that not any of Frederic's novels would prove quite worthy of the man, or be in any respect characteristic of his great humanity and remarkable humor, he nevertheless found that the first hundred pages of *Illumination* "carried the reader away on a broad full tide of such narration as adorns 'Rhoda Fleming,' and is not to be found in any other English novel."[13] Harris wrote this comment in his Frederic obituary two years after he had read the book, and for this reason it is clear that he sought to be restrained in his evaluation. It seemed to him that all Frederic's novels contained more than merely workmanlike construction and all revealed a distinct development of power in artistic achievement. But in *Illumination* he said that Frederic had come close to writing one of the truly great books in the English language—and certainly in the first hundred pages. Very likely at that point Harris became enamored of Celia Madden who, he thought, "tore the book to pieces" by pulling the reader's interest away from the other characters. Nevertheless, his estimate was only a little less extravagant than the estimates of most of his fellow journalists.[14]

Nor did Frederic lose stature after his most significant effort had been published and read. Even his fantasy, *March Hares,* won some plaudits. As has been noted, he published this book under his pseudonym, George Forth, in order not to detract from *Illumination,* which came out in the same year. But although the lighter work in no way compares with Theron Ware's story, the reviewer on the *Critic* staff wrote that in *March Hares* Frederic had freed himself from the onus of belonging to any one school of literature, that he had in fact made a declaration of literary independence.

If he had so far revealed himself as an exponent of Mr. Howells' realism, in this work at least he had relaxed into a kind of light humor and had written in any but a realistic vein.

Moreover, both *Gloria Mundi* and *The Market-Place,* though in some respects inferior to *Illumination,* still brought Frederic posthumous fame. Soon after his death and after a long list of obituaries had been published, his name, however, dropped rapidly from the pages of the English press. He was, after all, an American: most of his fictions had to do with Americans and the American scene. Such of his contemporaries as Aaron Watson, Robert Steven, Mrs. T. P. O'Connor, and Frank Harris (when, years after his death, they wrote their memoirs) naturally recalled fondly the man who had played such an unusual role in their midst almost from the moment of his arrival in London. Yet, even then, it was more often the man they remembered, not the author. Nor does it appear that Frederic left his mark upon English writers who followed in the wake of the burgeoning realistic movement of the early twentieth century.

II *The American Assessment*

With a few notable exceptions, American critics have over the past seventy-five years neglected Harold Frederic, either oversimplifying their study of him by considering chiefly *Seth's Brother's Wife* and *The Damnation of Theron Ware,* or relegating him to an ignominious obscurity from which he has only recently been recovered. In its day, of course, *The Damnation* flashed into exciting even if brief prominence, as has been noted. But for the most part, from the outset of his career, critics did not often urge Frederic upon American readers. And there can be no question that Frederic fretted over his failure to achieve a popular American market. He attributed that failure, in part, to what he considered inadequate promotion given him by his publishers. He wrote to Charles Scribner:

> I don't like to complain, but I *do* feel keenly that men who do work much inferior to mine get advantages in advertising . . . which my books, poor devils, may not hope for. I see

> your advertisements in a number of different forms, notably in *The Nation,* the magazines & the N. Y. papers. It may be all illusion on my part, but I seem to get less show in these than any other writer whose name is on your books. Even when *The Boston Herald* started a boom for 'In the Valley,' I heard of it from eight or ten strangers who wrote me from different parts of New England, but I could not learn that my publishers had lifted a finger to utilize the thing. . . .[15]

Charles Scribner tried to reassure him in a reply:

> We never worked harder over any books than we did over 'In the Valley' and 'The Lawton Girl' and yet their sale was not proportionate to our efforts. You, of course, will recognize that taste of the public in these matters is altogether capricious and the success of the inferior books is really due, not to any effort of the publishers, but because they happen to please the public fancy.[16]

Mr. Scribner was undoubtedly right. Roger Burlingame wrote that in the decade of the 1890's "there seemed to be a definite retrogression in the seriousness of fiction from those immediately preceding it. The promise of realism suggested by the regional novels of Hamlin Garland and Harold Frederic, the public of the Nineties was willing to leave unfulfilled. *Looking Backward,* Edward Bellamy's probing into the evils of capitalism, stood high in 1888; his *Equality* in 1897 (the most serious of the 90's) got nowhere near best-sellerdom. Instead there was a flood of romance, humor, and what we, today, consider the most saccharine of 'sob' sentimentality."[17]

Mr. Burlingame was looking backward from the firmer perspective of 1946. But Howells himself, in his *Criticism and Fiction* (1891), stated that the American novel of his day was not written for men and married women chiefly, as was the European novel, but for ladies especially and most of these young girls.[18] It was unlikely that the strong realism of *The Lawton Girl* or later *The Damnation of Theron Ware* would find favor in the bosoms of romantic young females whose appetites were more easily tempted by such honeyed stuff as *When Knighthood Was in Flower.*

It was, therefore, not only a lack of promotion on the part of Frederic's publishers nor only the unappreciative critics that accounted for Frederic's inability to achieve outstanding success. Yet no one can doubt, in reviewing the kind of critical opinion of his work circulated in this country during the 1880's and 1890's, that a considerably more favorable press might have stimulated a larger reading public. It may of course be that the critics themselves were swayed by popular taste, or that they catered to it.

As it was, one American (*Nation*) reviewer found *The Lawton Girl* "rather dingy reading," a sort of "industrious and idle apprentice type of novel," and exclaimed that since Frederic had in the end let his villains go unpunished he ought forever to have them on his conscience.[19] In a somewhat better vein, another *Nation* reviewer believed that *In the Valley* worked a fresh field for a novel and congratulated Frederic upon it. But the fainter praise that must have damned the book in Frederic's eyes, even if it tempted young ladies, was appended at the conclusion of the reviewer's comment: "His love story is a very pretty one, and in fine it must be said that the book may boast the non-negative merit in an historic novel of being nowhere a bore."[20]

Still another *Nation* reviewer stated that the force and interest in *Theron Ware* lay in its treatment of "the seamy side of creed and dogma." But though the conversation was applauded as brilliantly conceived, the review concluded with a back-of-the-hand comment: "The story, however, leads nowhither, and the reader is advised to make the most of the panorama as it passes."[21] If Frederic was disturbed and angered by this slighting review (and it is quite apparent that he followed the reviewing columns closely), he must have been elated with the comment of Harry Thurston Peck, one of the more perceptive critics of his day, who wrote in *The Bookman* (New York) for June, 1896, that *The Damnation of Theron Ware* was in his judgment a "distinctly great novel"; that Frederic had used his materials as William Dean Howells had only once or twice succeeded in doing.

But Frederic died a few months short of seeing perhaps the best of the contemporary American comments on his work, the one appearing in *The Atlantic Monthly* in April, 1899. By way of introduction to a review of *Gloria Mundi*, the critic wrote: "Of all the younger novelists of the day, save one [probably Stephen Crane], Frederic seemed to give the most virile and splendid promise. His was the most varied and precocious knowledge of life, the broadest range of sympathy, the most striking power of synthesis. There were masterly touches even in the earliest and crudest of his efforts; in *The Copperhead*, for example. There was the gathered and controlled power which compels attention even to its least pleasant manifestations, in the strong and singular tale which we like so much better to call *Illumination* than by its rather brutal American title, *The Damnation of Theron Ware*. But the author's own thought had clarified when he died. . . . Already, in *Illumination,* Frederic saw life with surprising steadiness. He seemed to be on the sure way to seeing it 'whole.' "[22]

Taking the good with the bad, however, Frederic did not fare so well as he might with American critics and reviewers of his day. Nor did he fare much better with his reading public. In fact, it is quite clear that the name died almost with the man; for with the exception of only an occasional comment, Frederic's name and his work did not reappear in this country for well over two decades following his death. Several of his books such as *The Return of the O'Mahony* and *Gloria Mundi,* the latter under the title of *Pomps and Vanities,* were reprinted in paperback by Heinemann in London as late as 1913. With possibly one exception, no record of such reprints could be found in the United States until the mid-thirties.

However, with the stirring of national pride brought on by World War I and with the subsequent gradual rise of the study of American literature in college and high school classrooms, a re-examination of the works of American authors commenced. Ultimately, Frederic was brought under the cold light of critical scrutiny; but no extended evaluation appeared until the publication of the third—and uncompleted—volume of Vernon Louis Parrington's *Main Currents of American Thought.* Mr. Parrington's rather oversimplified views about Frederic have been followed scrupulously, and perhaps uncritically, by many scholars of American literature since his time (see Chapter IV, *Seth's Brother's Wife*). But it is perhaps unfair to judge the uncompleted work of a man who so profoundly affected the opinions of American critics after *Main Currents* was published. Mr. Parrington went no further than *Seth* for his evaluation of Frederic; but had he lived to finish his study, he might have changed his mind even about *Seth,* to say nothing of how he might have dealt with *Theron Ware.* Nevertheless, Mr. Paul Haines was correct in his refutation of the Parrington thesis: namely, that the Parrington viewpoint is "wrong in detail and in its whole drift. . . ," for it ignored the best features of *Seth* and failed to recognize the characteristically American humor of the worldly and mature mind that created the novel.[23]

The truth is (and again Mr. Haines was correct in his statement) that a whole group of critics followed the Parrington thesis without giving the Frederic canon an adequate reading. This group assumed unequivocally that Frederic was bent on revealing American farm and small-town life as bringing about the spiritual impoverishment of farmer and townsman—a thought, as has been seen already, which was farthest from his mind as he wrote *Seth* or *The Lawton Girl* or *The Damnation of Theron Ware.*

But in more recent years, other critics, somewhat better informed about the Frederic books, even if they have not read Frederic thoroughly, have ventured different viewpoints. One of these has taken the position that while Frederic was certainly damning the farm and the small town, when he "was frustrated by his inability to sustain a naturalistic technique . . . this frustration turned into rage at his unmanageable materials, and that . . . rage expressed itself in the moral indignation which he directed at his characters."[24] Another critic has stated that in the varied phases of naturalism in American fiction, one can discover in Mark Twain and Harold Frederic, at least, both "moral confusion and dismay."[25]

It may well be that among all the latter-day critics, Mr. Everett Carter has come as close to the truth of Frederic's intent as any other; and though Mr. Carter, like almost all of Frederic's critics, concerned himself with *Seth* and *Ware* only, one finds in his statements that hard core of meaning that is at once Frederic's own conception of life and his literary expression of that conception. For he sees in both Seth and Theron Ware "the fall of the individual from innocence to disturbing knowledge"; that an "advance in knowledge . . . could be made at the expense of inner stability; there were primitive emotional balances which could not be disturbed without the danger of unsettling the entire personality, without danger of damning the soul." "*A Hazard of New Fortunes*," Mr. Carter continues, "was, in part, a story of the social fall of America; *The Damnation of Theron Ware* reached out to become a representation of the psychic fall of Americans. Like Americans in general, Theron Ware rose from ignorance to knowledge, and yet the rise was, at the same time, a disaster, a tragedy. . . ."[26]

It should be remembered, of course, that Mr. Carter's treatment of Frederic is only incidental to his longer study of William Dean Howells. Aside from the unpublished though stimulating work of Mr. Paul Haines and the more recent dissertation of Mr. Robert Woodward, Mr. John Henry Raleigh has undertaken the only expanded analysis of any single Frederic work. As might be expected, this is of *The Damnation of Theron Ware*. Mr. Raleigh states his intention as follows: "If *The Damnation* is unique in structure and psychology, it is unique as a cultural document as well. It exists on three historical and cultural levels: first, it emanates very clearly from late nineteenth-century America; second, it is also concerned with the perennial theme of much serious American literature: what is the identity and the nature of 'the American' and what is his relationship to Europe; and, third, it is a metaphysical statement about the essential polarities of all human existence."[27] Mr. Raleigh's statement is much too complex for mere summary; it is significant in that it represents one of the first attempts on the part of modern scholars to deal with Harold Frederic as a serious artist on the American scene. That a number of dissertations concerned with Frederic as a writer are now in progress is testimony to the rising tide of interest in the man, his work, and his place in American letters.

III *Frederic and His Contemporaries*

Like Henry James, Harold Frederic had the unusual experience among American writers of witnessing life on two continents. But there the resemblance ends. Frederic was always, it seems, essentially American even if his friend Frank Harris thought he had run away from his home state because he had grown tired of the daily chronicling of small beer. It is obvious that he never became English either in sentiment or in political ideology though he came to love England and the English, as well as the Irish, people.[28] James, on the other hand, was a hybrid: he lost almost all his American coloring during his long years in England and on the Continent; but he never became distinctly English or continental as an individual. Frederic was thrown headlong into English, Irish, and continental politics and commerce and became absorbed in problems largely international in scope. At the same time, while living in London and its suburbs chiefly, he consorted with the best known journalists, writers, and artists of his day. James was engrossed in his life work as a writer and was concerned, as Frederic seems to have believed, especially with literature and life in the parlor. In fact, Frederic once slurringly remarked: "Henry James is an effeminate old donkey who lives with a herd of other donkeys around him and insists on being treated as if he were the Pope. He has licked the dust from the floor of every third rate hostess in England. . . ."[29] Given the opportunity, James could likely have replied as caustically. But for all that, both men could look back, in their different ways, at the America they had for different reasons left behind.

Some advantages accrue to the writer who leaves his native land and experiences an enforced acculturation. A subtle shift in perspective, even a broader and larger perspective, is one of these. Remaining too close to an object, one may have only an oblique and limited view of it. For that reason, Frederic's removal to England served him well. Quite by chance, as has been noted, he was inspired in England to try his hand at a full-length novel; and, having already seen a good deal of the way people lived both in England and on the continent, he could view with a less biased eye the lives of his characters in Dearborn County, in Thessaly, Octavius, Tecumseh and Tyre. He could regard critically the conflict between, as well as the amalgamation of, the old and the new world cultures. Without a firm comprehension of that conflict, he might never have produced his worldly Father

Forbes nor his Burne-Jones-tinted figure, Celia Madden; nor would the pure science of Dr. Ledsmar have become understandable to him. In fact, he might never have produced with quite the same brilliance and seeming casualness his remarkable Sister Soulsby.

Even with his rich endowment of humor and his propensity for the ironic touch, the acquisition of a more cosmopolitan range and scope made it possible for him to create the gay mockery of British manners and customs to be found in his observations about Philistia in *Mrs. Albert Grundy.* Inspired perhaps by his already broad knowledge of the American-Irish in upstate New York, he sought to know their native Ireland too. Thus *The Return of the O'Mahony* has not only a sureness of treatment, it has also the larger comprehension of Irish history, Irish character, and Irish problems. So closely in tune was he with all things Irish, in fact, that even his dialect is said to have been phonetically almost perfect as he represented the speech of Erin's sons and daughters in the several fictions where they appear.

Had Frederic been unable to send out at least some feeder roots following his transplantation, he would never have been of such value as he was to the New York *Times.* In considering him as an author, one is prone to overlook the bread-and-butter income that he earned by meeting the deadlines for weekly dispatches to his paper. One may forget, too, the vastly significant business in which he was engaged: the meetings with men of influence on an international scale; with men engaged in the building of empires—financial, industrial, and commercial. If Frederic did not know State Street in Boston or Wall Street in New York, he knew Fleet Street and the Strand and High Holborn in London. Assuredly he was familiar with the comings and goings at Number 10 Downing Street; and for eight of the fourteen years that he spent in England (1885-89 and 1893-97), he had direct access to the White House through his good friends President Cleveland and the President's private secretary, Daniel S. Lamont. Few men of that day, or any day, not themselves political, diplomatic, or financial figures, could be so favorably advantaged as was Frederic as foreign correspondent of the New York *Times.* Few men, so advantaged, have developed so rapidly the intellectual grasp and the perception of both men and affairs that Frederic developed in his brief life with the English people.

Still, expatriation for a writer is not always a clear gain. To some extent Frederic lost his identity as an American author on the American scene. He lost opportunities to come into close contact with other American writers; for although he corresponded briefly with Gelett Burgess and Hamlin Garland and William Dean Howells and in England was for nearly two years associated with Stephen Crane, the evidence so far examined does not point to an intimate relationship with any other significant American author of the eighties or nineties. These factors may or may not have proved a handicap to Frederic; they are difficult to evaluate in his total output of fiction. But the expatriate artist suffers another kind of loss that cannot be undervalued: that is, the loss of contact with indigenous materials for his creative efforts. Other men have learned, even in more recent times, that while leaving the homeland means a gain in perspective it may also mean a shift in the frame of artistic reference. So it proved true with Henry James. So, today, it has proved true with Ernest Hemingway.

That is precisely what happened to Harold Frederic. The sometimes expressed complaint that he wrote too hurriedly, that he was forced by circumstances to create potboilers, that because he was facile he was careless and did not think things through cannot be justified. While it is true that he had many mouths to feed in both London and Kenley, and needed money badly, it is altogether possible that he had written himself out of his American scene and character. *The Damnation of Theron Ware,* which was published in 1896, had actually been completed a year earlier; and even then it had gone through a gestation period of five years before Frederic brought it to birth. Moreover, in the collection of notes and half-completed manuscripts remaining to us today in the Frederic Collection of the Library of Congress is evidence that he had no intention of returning to the Mohawk Valley as a backdrop for his fictions.

The enforced transplantation and all that it meant to Frederic in his creative work has made the problem of a fair assessment difficult. More complicated still is finding the proper place for him among his contemporaries. The tendency so far has been toward an oversimplification, as we have noted: namely, that Frederic made a significant contribution to the progress of realism, a statement that is acceptably safe; or that he moved toward naturalism and a deterministic concept of life—a statement that is not adequately supported by the evidence.

To be specific, one may say that Frederic obviously knew Mrs. Ward's *Robert Elsmere* (1888), that he may have known Margaret Deland's *John Ward, Preacher* (though this latter is by no means certain), and that he built on the substantial ground of realism they had cultivated, nurturing its cause in *Theron Ware*. However, that Frederic's Joel Thorpe became the prototype for Norris' Curtis Jadwin in *The Pit*, or for Dreiser's Frank Cowperwood in *The Financier*, or even for London's Burning Daylight in his novel by that name, does not at all follow. For one thing, the financial wizard capable of somewhat shady manipulations was already well known to Americans in the figures of Ames and Gould and Fisk. Frederic may have drawn Thorpe after their pattern. For another thing, Norris was concerned with an epic of wheat; Jadwin is incidental to his total study. London drew Burning Daylight from his own experiences in the Klondike. Dreiser, by his own admission, modeled his Cowperwood after Charles T. Yerkes, whose exploits in the financial and political world made him an apt hero for a Dreiser novel. No simple formula is applicable to this period during which Frederic marketed his literary wares.

Actually, a conglomerate of fiction appeared. In the United States, in the vanguard of realism one finds Kirkland's *Zury: The Meanest Man in Spring County* and *The McVeys;* Howells' *A Hazard of New Fortunes*, among a number of his novels of lesser significance; Margaret Deland's *John Ward, Preacher* and *Philip and his Wife;* Garland's *Main-Traveled Roads* and *Rose of Dutcher's Coolly;* and Crane's *Maggie* and *The Red Badge of Courage*. At the same time, one sees such romantic novels as Eggleston's *The Graysons;* Burnett's *Little Lord Fauntleroy* and *A Lady of Quality;* and Davis' *Soldiers of Fortune*. Along with Bellamy (*Looking Backward*), Howells identified himself as a writer of Utopian idealism in his *A Traveler from Altruria* (1894). But these, perhaps the best of the works published, are no more than representative of a vast bulk of fictions that appeared.

In England, a close parallel can be found for the American product. Among the realistic novels, one finds Hardy's *Tess* and *Jude the Obscure* heading the list; Meredith's *The Amazing Marriage,* Mrs. Ward's *Robert Elsmere* and *Marcella,* Gissing's *The Emancipated* and *New Grub Street,* and George Moore's *Esther Waters* and *Evelyn Innes* accompany Hardy with varying degrees of realism. In the romantic vein, Robert Louis Stevenson's *The Black Arrow* and *The Master of Ballantrae* are markedly superior to the trivial, even though popular, *She* and *Allan Quartermain* of Rider Haggard, and *The Prisoner of Zenda* and *Rupert of Hentzau* of Anthony Hope. William Morris' half-fantasy, half-Utopian romance, notably as one finds it in *The House of the Wolfings, The Story of the Glittering Plain,* and *The Well at the World's End,* moves toward but is not so closely identified with Bellamy's Utopia as is his *News from Nowhere.*

Thus one may see that during Frederic's productive years no "school" of fiction prevailed. Fantasy, romance, realism, Utopian idealism and other forms of social criticism—all these could be found in the bookseller's shop. But, in fact, if any held sway, one must concede, in looking at the record, that it was romance, historical and otherwise; that the writers of realistic or naturalistic novels, with extremely rare exceptions, found their footing along the highway of literature precarious and their progress beset at every turning with the obstacle of popular resistance.

Mr. Howells could well admonish American novelists: remember, he wrote in 1891, "that there is no greatness, no beauty, which does not come from truth to your own knowledge of things; and keep on working, even if your work is not long remembered."[30] Perhaps he should have amended the last to read: "even if your work is not purchased or read." *That* would have been closer to the facts that he himself recognized. He complained that American writers had no urge to deal with nakedness or with the harsher realities of life. "But," he continued, "they ask why, when the conventions of the plastic and histrionic arts liberate their followers to the portrayal of almost any phase of the physical or of the emotional nature, an American novelist may not write a story on the lines of Anna Karenina or Madame Bovary. Sappho they put aside, and from Zola's work they avert their eyes. They do not condemn him or Daudet. . . . But they do sometimes wish to do another kind, to touch one of the most serious and sorrowful problems of life in the spirit of Tolstoi and Flaubert, and they ask why they may not."[31] One should recall here what has already been said about the difficulty Hardy had with both public and critics over the publication of his greatest fictions. Not so well established or so well known as Hardy, George Gissing and George Moore met resistance in a less conspicuous way. Nor should one forget how, at the turn of the century, George Bernard Shaw was forced to abandon his less pleasant plays and salvage his career by a generous application of Irish-frosted wit and laughter to his more serious efforts.

Somehow, this struggle of the realists for recognition and for the right to create according to their own artistic principles and desires has in these latter days been underestimated and undervalued. It is a truism that in any age new art forms meet the sternest kind of opposition. If they persist and if they have value, they ultimately come to be understood and accepted. But as the struggle for their existence recedes into the forgotten pages of our histories of art and literature, the scholar-critic tends, in his re-examination of the work of the several artists involved, to fix and formulate and classify. No one can deny either the desirability of or the necessity for this re-examination and re-evaluation.

But Harold Frederic simply refuses to be fixed, formulated, and classified. In the light of his total production, it is impossible to align him finally with Garland or Howells, or, as has more often been the case with critics who have considered his work, with Stephen Crane and Frank Norris.

To be sure, one may find in Stephen Crane both realistic and naturalistic tendencies—the latter most notably in *Maggie* and in *The Open Boat*. But at the risk of making an almost too broad generalization, one may say that Crane possessed a rare genius in a limited area of creativity. He was essentially the impressionist in his best work, writing in the realistic manner. He was, in one sense, a disciple of Mr. Howells' precept that a writer should remain true to himself, should create fictions with an eye to the truth always in mind. Frank Norris, on the other hand, was at once both romantic and realistic or naturalistic; one may contrast *A Man's Woman* and *McTeague,* for example. He seems to have been confused himself as to the precise meanings of these terms; and he nowhere so naïvely revealed his confusion as in his chapter, "A Plea for Romantic Fiction," in his *The Responsibilities of a Novelist.* "Romance," he wrote, ". . . is the kind of fiction that takes cognizance of variations from the type of normal life. Realism is the kind of fiction that confines itself to the normal life."[32] Thus, Zola, according to his definition, should be classed as a romanticist. "Realism . . . ," he continued, "need not be in the remotest sense or degree offensive, but on the other hand respectable as a church and proper as a deacon—as, for instance, the novels of Mr. Howells."[33]

With theorizing of this kind Harold Frederic had almost nothing to do, at least where the written record is concerned. Nor did he confine himself to one pattern or style. He ran the gamut, utilizing nearly every form that his own age produced. To associate him, therefore, with a particular group of writers, or to place him in any but the most general of relationships with his age would be to force upon him a kind of literary *mariage de convenance.* He wrote what he thought he should write; and in some instances, no doubt, he wrote what he thought would find a good market. He should be identified, then, with the proper people at the proper time, if identification is to be insisted upon. When he wrote *Seth* and *The Lawton Girl* and *The Damnation of Theron Ware,* along with his collection of Civil War stories, he was a realist after the manner of Garland and Crane, or perhaps after the manner of Hardy and George Moore. When he wrote historical romance, he was, even as he saw himself, following the pattern of Thackeray. For *The Return of the O'Mahony* and *March Hares* he was beholden to no one, unless in his humor he had caught something of the spirit of W. E. Henley and Bernard Partridge and in his whimsy had discovered the soul of James M. Barrie. With *Gloria Mundi* he became half social commentator and half romancer—and almost without a model. In *The Market-Place* he was essentially the satirist.

That he wanted to succeed as an author cannot be doubted. Yet if his success is to be measured by the volume of the sale of his books, he was not markedly successful. One explanation for this fact lay unquestionably in the general lag in enthusiasm for realistic fiction in the nineties. For although *Theron Ware* found a high place on the list of best sellers for 1896, replacing *The Red Badge of Courage*, it was even then outstripped by more trivial books and fell off rapidly.

But other reasons may be found, a number of the most cogent of these pointed up by one of Frederic's British contemporaries.[34] For one, Frederic was neither a good businessman nor a bargainer. He wrote no letters to editors of magazines in which his books were reviewed. He did not seek out some notable of the day to write a preface for any of his works, a device that helped to bring recognition and even wealth to lesser men. He did not judge his markets accurately. For example, when he wrote *The Return of the O'Mahony*, Parnell was already dead, his reputation destroyed. Home Rule, on which Frederic had written so brilliantly for the *Times*, was no longer an issue before Parliament. Only *Ware* and *The Market-Place* moved into the realm of best sellerdom, the former probably because of its subject, the latter probably because it had been serialized in *The Saturday Evening Post* and so had a ready-made reputation. Even then, Frederic was not to enjoy the brief success of his last book, for it was published posthumously.

But for all that, the current resurgence of interest in Harold Frederic is testimony to the durable quality of his fiction. He has been rediscovered. Today, one may say that *The Damnation of Theron Ware* is considerably more than a minor classic and is not by any means the only readable, even if it is the most significant, book that Frederic wrote. Howells' *The Rise of Silas Lapham* and *A Modern Instance*, despite the skill exhibited in their execution, are pale beside *Ware* or *Seth*. The names of Kirkland and Garland and Fuller, yes, and Norris, too, are all but forgotten. Frederic had substance. The promise that he displayed in *Seth*, whatever crudities in it may be complained against, he lived up to in succeeding fictions. *Ware* was clearly the work of genius that only needed time for development. Skill and power were there. The broader canvas, the deeper plumbing of character, the higher finish in structure and style—these surely would have come had he not been stricken in mid-career.

As it is, Harold Frederic's stature among latter nineteenth-century American writers is today being recognized. He is taking his place, like Stephen Crane, in the vanguard of writers of that time. Though he did not possess all the natural endowments that Crane exhibited, he had many compensating facets of personality, among these a rich good humor that Crane did not often display. Crane had the greater artistry; Frederic had the greater warmth and human understanding. Crane had a vision of life and created its image; Frederic, perhaps lacking Crane's subtlety, saw life in the round and portrayed it that way. Crane was a man haunted, confused, and driven. Frederic had the vast hunger for life, and he lived it joyously and to the full.

Frederic had the marks of greatness on him. His books reveal him as impetuous and headstrong on the one hand, yet sensitive, compassionate, and highly imaginative on the other. One should keep in mind the fact that if he grew to young manhood in the small-town and rural atmosphere of upstate New York and was the companion of small-town newsmen and politicians, he lived to become the intimate of many of the truly great figures of his generation, the object of their admiration and affection. In fourteen brief years, along with his compelling duties to the New York *Times,* he wrote nearly a dozen novels and novelettes, an impressive number of short stories and sketches, a biography, and a long list of articles about an equally long list of subjects. The Harold Frederic Collection in the Library of Congress makes one think that his creative imagination was never at rest. His works and notes reveal, too, that if he was without much formal schooling, he disciplined and tutored himself in every useful area of learning. For him, life itself was a book, its contents to be devoured in great gulps. Such a man was Harold Frederic, journalist and author.

Notes and References

Chapter One

1. Frederic's birthplace, numbered 56 South Street in 1856, still stands (1960), although it is now numbered 324 South.

2. See *Van Rensselaer Bouwier Manuscripts* (Albany, 1908), p. 807. "Henrich frerixsen van bunnick, 26 years old," directed the Patroon, Kiliaen van Rensselaer, in his own handwriting, "shall receive 120 guilders a year and a pair of boots in four years and as a gratuity for the passage [from Holland to the colony of New Netherland] 25 guilders" (*ibid.*, p. 196). This first Henry Frederick (to Anglicize his name) came from Bunnick, a small town near Utrecht; he eventually became a foreman on the farm managed for the Patroon by Gerrit Theusen de Reux.

3. See *The Palatines of New York State* (published by the Palatine Society of the United Evangelical Lutheran Church, 1953), p. 53 and *passim*. See also, Hardin and Willard, *History of Herkimer County* (Syracuse, 1893).

4. For evidence that Captain Mark Damuth fought in and survived the battle of Oriskany on August 6, 1777, see the roster reproduced in Allen C. Beach (ed.), *Centennial Celebrations of the State of New York* (Albany, 1879), p. 145.

5. "Preface to a Uniform Edition," *In the Sixties* (New York, 1897), p. vi.

6. See *New York in the Revolution* (Albany, 1904), I, 52, where he is listed as "Moses Randle." His settlement in Utica is mentioned in Moses M. Bagg, *Pioneers of Utica* (Utica, 1892), p. 229. He is also listed, although no address is given, in the first Utica *Directory* (1817).

7. See Paul Haines, "Harold Frederic" (unpubl. diss., New York University, 1945), p. 8. Haines gathered this and much other factual information from Frederic's relatives still living in Utica in the 1930's.

8. *Ibid.*

9. Haines (p. 10) quotes Frederic's daughter, Mrs. Eliot Keen, to the effect that "to the end of his days Harold . . . remembered the exceeding harshness of his mother's voice."

10. For this detail, see *What Do You Know About Utica,* a pamphlet published in May, 1927, pp. 57-58.

11. See Nelson Greene, *History of the Mohawk Valley* (Chicago, 1925), IV, 378.

12. The Utica *Directory* for 1861-62 lists "Frederick, Frances, widow of H. D., 56 South." For 1862-63 the entry for 56 South is "DeMott, Wm." There is no entry for 1863-64, but for 1864-65 it is "DeMott, Wm. H., machinist." See also Haines, p. 8.

13. Haines (p. 11) cites Baxter family tradition for this detail. Matilda Ramsdell, Frederic's aunt, married John Baxter. Their descendants flourished in Utica for two generations.

14. Evidence about the kind of books available to Frederic in his boyhood home is found in a copy of *The Damnation of Theron Ware* (thirty-sixth thousand; Chicago, 1899) carefully annotated in 1920 by one of his Baxter cousins. On page 92 of this volume, now in the present writers' possession, this entry is penciled in the margin: "My grandmother's book. Here he [Frederic] makes himself Theron." This note appears next to the list of books in Theron Ware's library, and refers specifically to "a copy of 'Josephus' which had belonged to his [Ware's] grandmother, and had seen him through many a weary Sunday afternoon in his boyhood."

15. For William Frederick's part in the founding of the Corn Hill ME Church, later known as the South Street Church, see H. Paul Draheim, "Free Methodist Parish Grew from Dissent," Utica *Observer-Dispatch,* January 26, 1952.

16. *Ibid.*

17. For a brief but sympathetic account of Seymour's career, with emphasis on his bid for the Presidency in 1868, see Irving Stone, *They Also Ran* (New York, 1946), pp. 266-85.

18. The Utica *Directory* for 1867-68 contains this entry: "Wm. H. DeMoth [*sic*], woodyard, Dudley and Seymour, house 56 South." Not until 1872 does the entry read "wood and milk dealer," although the dairy was part of the business before this. In an interview printed in *The Bookman,* III (July, 1896), 384, Frederic is quoted as saying: "I was brought up on or near a farm." This inaccurate statement later confused commentators. He was more nearly accurate when he continued: "I spent my boyhood in getting out of bed at five in the morning to look at cattle, and until I was fourteen I drove a 'milk wagon' as a 'side issue' in my agricultural duties."

19. The Advanced School is described in Bagg, *Memorial History of Utica,* p. 467.

20. Frederic's claim that he had read these books before he was six must be discounted, as Haines points out (p. 12.). They were available to him, however, as were the other books listed here,

in the Utica School District Library, according to its *Catalogue* for 1875.

21. Quoted in Robert H. Sherard, "Harold Frederic," *The Idler,* XII (1897), 531-40. Emile Erckmann (1822-1899) and Alexandre Chatrian (1826-1890) began their long career as collaborators in 1847, although their first major success did not arrive until 1859, with *The Illustrious Dr. Mathews.* For Frederic's own acknowledgment of his debt to Erckmann-Chatrian, see "Preface to a Uniform Edition," *In the Sixties,* p. x.

22. See the Utica *Observer* for January 23, 26, and 29, 1878.

23. Haines (p. 14), from interviews with Arthur Pflanz in December, 1934, and August, 1935, and with Wally Hill, a schoolmate of Frederic's, in August, 1935. The portrait of Von Moltke, according to Haines, "is dull but not bad or childish." In 1935 the portrait was in the possession of the Baxters.

24. "Preface to a Uniform Edition," p. vi.

25. *The Annual Report of the Utica Public Schools, 1870-71* contains (pp. 58-70) a complete list of "questions submitted to pupils of the graduating class of each grade at the annual examinations, July, 1871." The story of the commencement exercises appears in the Utica *Morning Herald and Daily Gazette* for Friday, July 7, 1871. Haines points out that the commencement play in which Frederic had a role seems to contain an anticipatory echo of Dr. Ledsmar's description of his Chinese servant in *Ware,* pp. 120-21. The play was entitled "Fing Wing, Coming Man."

Chapter Two

1. Descriptions of Mundy's flourishing establishment appear in numerous contemporary area publications, including the *Atlas of Oneida County* (Philadelphia, 1874), p. 111, and the Utica *Directory* for 1877, p. 63.

2. Haines, p. 15.

3. The history of the Adjutant Bacon Cadets and references to their activities may be found in a number of places, including Durant, *History of Oneida County,* p. 340 and pp. 346-47; the *Utica Saturday Globe* for August 25, 1900; and the Utica *Directory* for 1877. The caricature described here is reproduced in the Utica *Observer-Dispatch,* February 17, 1957, p. 7-A.

4. Baxter, p. 10. In the opening chapter of *Ware,* Frederic describes the lodgings to which the visiting Bishop has been assigned during his stay in Tecumseh. Baxter's penciled note in the margin indicates that Frederic is describing "Aunt Frank's house," i.e., Frances Frederic DeMott's house.

5. Details of the Conference may be found in *Minutes of Northern New York Annual Conference of the Methodist Episcopal Church, Held in Utica, April 16-22, 1873* (Watertown, 1873), *passim.* Bishop Peck's remarks are reported on p. 29.

6. See Haines, p. 16, for a brief, factual account of Frederic's sojourn in Boston.

7. The phrase "Boston talkers" appears in *In the Valley* (p. 123), and is applied specifically to Fisher Ames. Frederic's attitude toward New England generally is obvious throughout this novel, and in some of his editorials. See, for example, the editorial in the Albany *Journal* for October 23, 1882.

8. Haines, p. 18.

9. Samuel Durant, *History of Oneida County* (Philadelphia, 1878), p. 303.

10. *Ibid.*, p. 297.

11. The manuscript of "The Jew's Christmas" may be presumed extant, but it was not available to the present writers. Haines, who read the manuscript, says that "the style has an easy expedience of syntax and a promising fullness of detail, obvious indeed, but flowing readily from the pen" (p. 28).

12. The manuscript of "The Story of Peter Zarl" is in the Harold Frederic Papers, the Library of Congress.

13. Frederic later reported that he was unable to join the Oneida Historical Society because he lacked the two dollars membership fee. (See "Preface to a Uniform Edition," pp. vi-vii.) Like the story that he was "expelled from school," this is a fiction; his name appears on the list of charter members of the Oneida Historical Society, Utica, N. Y.

14. *Harper's New Monthly Magazine,* LV (July, 1877), 171-83.

15. Utica *Observer*, June 16, 1877, p. 2.

16. Durant, *History of Oneida County,* p. 129.

17. *Ibid.*

18. "Preface to a Uniform Edition," p. vii. For a lengthier discussion of Frederic's lifelong admiration for Horatio Seymour, see Abe C. Ravitz, "Harold Frederic's Venerable Copperhead," *New York History,* XLI (January, 1960), 35-48.

19. In December, 1878, and in February, 1879, Frederic covered two particularly brutal and sordid murder cases for the *Observer*. Haines provides details about both (pp. 45-50).

20. See the Utica *Observer* for July 21 and 22, 1880. Frederic undoubtedly attended at least one of these picnics, which he describes in authentic detail in Chapters 22 and 23 of *The Damnation of Theron Ware*. The Methodist camp which he describes in Chapter 22 is still operated near the village of Trenton, N. Y.

21. *Ibid.*, June 30, 1879.
22. *Ibid.*, May 3, 1880.
23. *Ibid.*, April 5, 1880.
24. *Ibid.*, September 10 and 13, 1880.
25. See the *Observer*, June 19, 1882; June 21, 1882; and July 8, 1882.
26. *Ibid.*, August 31, 1882.
27. Allan Nevins, *Grover Cleveland: A Study in Courage* (New York, 1932), pp. 132-33.
28. The Boston *Herald* described Apgar as the man who "more than any other person, has shaped Democratic policies in New York for ten years. He has been known as the man who first directed the attention of the Democratic leaders to Mayor [of Buffalo] Cleveland, and, by the force of his personal influence, convinced Chairman Manning and other leaders who, in 1882 were disposed toward [Roswell] Flower, that the policy of the party demanded Cleveland's nomination for Governor." Quoted in *In Memoriam: Edgar Kelsey Apgar*, ed. Moses Coit Tyler (Ithaca, 1886), p. 115.
29. *In Memoriam: Edgar Kelsey Apgar*, pp. 137-38.
30. *Ibid.*, p. 141.
31. *Ibid.*, p. 135.
32. Haines, p. 122.

Chapter Three

1. *Memoirs of an Editor* (New York, 1924), pp. 279-80.
2. Letter from Mrs. Eliot Keen, August 4, 1960 (in possession of present writers).
3. From the original, now in the possession of Mr. Harold Frederic, Jr. Quoted by the permission of Mr. Frederic.
4. Haines, pp. 104-5.
5. New York *Times*, July 27, 1884, p. 1.
6. See Haines, pp. 110-11.
7. Quoted by the permission of the New York State Library at Albany from the original in the New York State Library at Albany.
8. (London, 1925), pp. 157-58.
9. See Haines, pp. 118-19.
10. "Harold Frederic—The Reminiscences of a Colleague," New York *Times*, October 23, 1898, p. 19.
11. *A Newspaper Man's Memories*, p. 158.
12. The best account of Frederic's reasons for resigning from the Savage is contained in Haines, pp. 173-74; Watson explains

the situation briefly in *Memories,* p. 163. In effect, Frederic had either been given or had purchased for £10 a copy of Swinburne's latest poems, yet to be published, and had telegraphed the entire contents to the United States. The original owner of the volume, Mr. E. St. John Brenon, another Savage member, reproached Frederic bitterly and the situation became tense. Frederic's friends advised him to withdraw from the club and he did so. Since the poems were not re-printed, at least not in the *Times,* the story is open to some question.

13. *Memories,* pp. 158-59.

14. Letter from Mrs. Keen, August 4, 1960.

15. Letter in the Papers of Grover Cleveland, the Library of Congress.

16. *Ibid.*

17. "Preface to a Uniform Edition," *In the Sixties,* pp. vii-viii.

18. Letter in the C. W. Barrett Collection. Quoted by the kind permission of Mr. Barrett.

19. Probably this was Maurice Barrymore, father of Lionel, Ethel, and John Barrymore, famous in American stage and movie history.

20. "Preface to a Uniform Edition," p. viii.

21. From handwritten copies of letters sent to Frederic, November 17, 1887 and January 16, 1890, London, in the files of Chatto and Windus.

22. At present Mr. Scribner's policy does not permit the correspondence of his company's authors to be reviewed.

23. Frederic returned to the United States only three times; thereafter, he remained in England, taking his vacations chiefly in Ireland.

24. "Harold Frederic—The Reminiscences of a Colleague," New York *Times,* October 23, 1898, p. 19.

25. "Harold Frederic, the Author of *The Market-Place,*" *Saturday Evening Post,* CLXXI (December 17, 1898), 396.

26. "Some Recollections of Harold Frederic," *Saturday Review,* LXXXVI (October 29, 1898), 571-72.

27. C. Lewis Hind, *More Authors and I* (London, 1922), p. 114.

28. *Ibid.*

29. "*The Sketch* Regrets the Loss to London of Mr. Harold Frederic," *The Sketch,* XXIV (October 26, 1898), 4.

30. Arthur Warren, "Harold Frederic—The Reminiscences of a Colleague," New York *Times,* October 23, 1898, p. 19.

31. *Memories,* pp. 157-58.

32. "*The Sketch* Regrets. . . ."

33. "Chronicle and Comment," *The Bookman,* III, no. 5 (July, 1896), 384.

34. Letters from Harold Frederic, Jr., May 30, June 8, June 27, 1960.

35. Appointment diaries in the Harold Frederic Papers, Library of Congress.

36. Letter from Mrs. Eliot Keen, August 6, 1960.

37. See Haines, pp. 158-59.

38. See Kelly's *Directories* for the years 1884-1900, Guildhall Library, London.

39. Interview with Barry Forman, June, 1959, and subsequent letters.

40. See letters of Kate Lyon to Stephen and Cora Crane, the Crane Collection, Butler Library, Columbia University.

41. Letters in C. W. Barrett Collection. Quoted here by the permission of Mr. Barrett.

42. See letters in the possession of Mr. Ames W. Williams, Alexandria, Virginia.

43. All three letters are to be found in the Harold Frederic Papers, the Library of Congress.

44. *Some More Memoirs* (London, 1924), p. 43.

45. See Haines, p. 227.

46. Letter from Mrs. Eliot Keen, August 4, 1960.

Chapter Four

I *Seth's Brother's Wife*

1. "Preface to a Uniform Edition," p. viii.

2. Frederic to John B. Howe. The letter, quoted earlier, is in the C. W. Barrett Collection.

3. Frederic to Lamont, April 24, 1886. Cleveland Papers, Library of Congress.

4. *Seth's Brother's Wife* ran in *Scribner's* from I (January, 1887) through II (November, 1887). The first number of the new magazine sold 100,000 copies, according to Roger Burlingame, *Of Making Many Books* (New York, 1946), p. 211.

5. Vernon Louis Parrington, *Main Currents in American Thought* (New York), III, p. 288.

6. Frederic to Howe, February 27, 1886. See Summation, p.

7. Frederic to Lamont, April 24, 1886.

8. Frederic to Cleveland, November 8, 1884. The Cleveland Papers, Library of Congress.

9. Haines, p. 168.

II *In the Valley*

1. "Preface to a Uniform Edition," p. viii.
2. *Ibid.*
3. See Nelson Greene, *History of the Mohawk Valley* (Chicago, 1925), IV, pp. 709-12, for this report in a brief but interesting biographical article about Frederic.
4. "Preface to a Uniform Edition," p. viii.
5. Quoted in Roger Burlingame, *Of Making Many Books* (New York, 1946), p. 5.
6. *In the Valley* ran in *Scribner's* from VI (September, 1889) through VIII (July, 1890).
7. Frederic to Cleveland, November 13, 1889. Cleveland Papers, Library of Congress.
8. *Harper's* LXII (October, 1890), 800.

III *The Lawton Girl*

1. "Preface to a Uniform Edition," p. viii.
2. Frederic to Howells, May 5, 1885. Reprinted by the permission of Harvard University Library and of the Frederic heirs.
3. See Richard Hofstadter, *Social Darwinism in American Thought* (Boston, 1955), p. 79. This book has excellent chapters on both Sumner and Ward.
4. "Preface to a Uniform Edition," p. ix.
5. Walter F. Taylor, *The Economic Novel in America* (Chapel Hill, 1942), p. 2. Reuben Tracy is appropriately fond of Carlyle. He has "an old collection of Carlyle's earlier essays, and . . . liked it better, perhaps, than any other member of his library family." Horace Boyce notes that "Reuben had come to know about Carlyle after everybody else had ceased reading him."
6. Quoted in Merle Curti, *The Growth of American Thought* (New York, 1943), p. 638.

IV *The Return of the O'Mahony*

1. "The Ireland of Today," by "X." *The Fortnightly Review*, LX (November, 1893), 686-706; The Rhetoricians of Ireland," by "X." *The Fortnightly Review*, LX (December, 1893), 713-27; "The Ireland of Tomorrow," by "X." *The Fortnightly Review*, LXI (January, 1894), 1-18.
2. Haines, p. 315.
3. Robert H. Woodward, "Harold Frederic: A Study of His Novels, Short Stories, and Plays" (unpubl. diss., Indiana University, 1957), p. 208.

V The Civil War Stories

1. "Preface to a Uniform Edition," p. x. The seven stories include "The Copperhead," "The Deserter," "Marsena," and "A Day in the Wilderness," which are novelettes; "The War Widow," "My Aunt Susan," and "The Eve of the Fourth." The stories are printed, in various combinations, in four different collections: *The Copperhead and Other Stories* (1894); *Marsena and Other Stories of the War Time* (1894); *In the Sixties* (1897); and *The Deserter and Other Stories* (1898).

2. *Ibid.*

3. *Ibid.*, ix-x.

4. Stephen Crane, "Harold Frederic," *The Chapbook,* VII (1898), 358-59.

5. Frederic's appointment diaries for 1891, 1892, and 1893 are in the Harold Frederic Papers, Library of Congress.

Chapter Five

1. Edwin Arlington Robinson to Harry DeForest Smith, October 15, 1896, in *Untriangulated Stars,* edited by Denham Sutcliffe (Cambridge, Mass., 1947), p. 258.

2. "London Letter" dated 17 April 1896, *The Critic,* XXV n.s. (May 2, 1896), 316.

3. *Ibid.*, p. 310.

4. *Bookman,* III (June, 1896), 351.

5. *Cosmopolitan,* XXI (August, 1896), 439.

6. *The Critic,* XXVI n.s. (September 12, 1896), 156.

7. *Bookman,* III (July, 1896), 469.

8. The best evidence of the contemporary success of *The Damnation of Theron Ware* is to be found in the "Book Mart" sections of *Bookman* for 1896 and 1897. In *Bookman* IV (October, 1896), 176-78, for example, *Ware* tops best-seller lists from Los Angeles, Portland, and St. Paul; it places second on lists from Chicago, Albany, Cincinnati, and Rochester; it is third on lists from New York and Philadelphia. Alice Payne Hackett gives it fifth place on her list of American best-sellers for 1896. See her *Sixty Years of Best Sellers* (New York, 1956), p. 96.

9. *The Critic,* XXV n.s. (May 2, 1896), 310.

10. The three "Prologues," one of them bearing the date "Oct. 17, 1890," are included in the mass of notes for *The Damnation of Theron Ware* to be found in the Harold Frederic Papers in the Library of Congress. These Prologues and what is probably the earliest cast of characters introduce a Roman Catholic bishop, a rural dean, and Father Charles Joyce, "a plodding young curate,"

as well as "The Rev. Vincent Forbes of St. Thomas Didymus, Octavius." Father Forbes was the only Catholic clergyman to survive Frederic's subsequent excisions of both episodes and characters. In Frederic's early plans, Theron Ware's wife's name was Agnes, "née Hastings"; her name was later changed to Alice.

11. *The Critic,* XXV (May 2, 1896), 310.

12. *Howells and the Age of Realism* (Philadelphia, 1954), p. 243.

Chapter Six

I *March Hares*—no notes.

II *Gloria Mundi*

1. The Harold Frederic Papers, Library of Congress.
2. *Ibid.*
3. *Ibid.*
4. *Ibid.*
5. *Ibid.*

III *The Market-Place*

1. A simple statement of Nietzsche's basic ideas can be found in Arthur Berndtson's "Vitalism," in *A History of Philosophical Systems* (New York, 1950), pp. 375-80. For extended statements one must, of course, turn to Nietzsche's books: *Thus Spake Zarathustra,* Parts 1-3 completed in 1883-1884, Part 4 in 1891; *Beyond Good and Evil* (1886), particularly the Ninth Article; and *The Genealogy of Morals* (1887).

2. "Pleasure is a feeling accompanying increase of power; but the value lies in the increase of power, not in the pleasure." See Berndtson, p. 379.

3. See *Beyond Good and Evil,* no. 259.
4. Berndtson, p. 379.
5. See *Beyond Good and Evil,* no. 272.
6. *Ibid.,* no. 293.
7. *Ibid.,* no. 293.

Chapter Seven

1. See his *Complete Writings,* XV (Hartford, 1904), pp. 157-58.
2. "Preface to a Uniform Edition," *In the Sixties,* p. viii.
3. Harold Frederic Papers, the Library of Congress.
4. Letter from Mrs. Eliot Keen, August 30, 1960.

5. Quoted by the permission of the Library of Harvard University.

6. Interview with one of the present writers, London, The National Liberal Club, May 21, 1959. Sir Alfred is at this time Vice-President of the National Liberal Club.

7. "The Lawton Girl," *The Athenaeum*, no. 3265 (May 24, 1890), 670.

8. "Novel Notes," *The Bookman* (London), VI (May, 1894), 56-58.

9. April, 1898, 405-6.

10. LXXVI (April 4, 1896). Quoted in London edition, Heinemann, 1896, i.

11. Quoted in London edition, Heinemann, 1896, i.

12. *Ibid.*

13. *The Saturday Review*, LXXXVI (October 22, 1898), 526-28.

14. *Ibid.*

15. See Roger Burlingame, *Of Making Many Books* (New York, 1946), pp. 116-17. Quoted by the permission of Scribner's and Sons, New York, and by the Frederic heirs.

16. *Ibid.*

17. *Ibid.*, p. 132.

18. (London, 1891), p. 149.

19. *The Nation*, LI (September 4, 1890), 195.

20. *The Nation*, LII (June 11, 1891), 483.

21. *The Nation*, LXIII (September 3, 1896), 181.

22. *The Atlantic Monthly*, LXXXIII (April, 1899), 522-24.

23. See Haines, pp. 256-76, *passim.*

24. Charles C. Walcutt, *American Literary Naturalism, A Divided Stream* (Minneapolis, 1956), p. 49.

25. Spiller, Thorp, *et al.*, *Literary History of the United States*, II (New York, 1948), p. 1016.

26. *Howells and the Age of Realism* (New York, 1950), pp. 241-44, *passim.*

27. *American Literature*, III, no. 2 (May, 1958), 213.

28. A close reading of the memoirs of Frederic's friends in England, of Frederic's letters to his contemporaries, and even of his notes in the Library of Congress, leads one to conclude that the longer Frederic remained in England the fonder of both the people and the country he became.

29. Thomas Beer, *Hanna, Crane, and The Mauve Decade* (New York, 1941), p. 321.

30. *Criticism and Fiction* (London, 1891), p. 145.

31. *Ibid.*, pp. 153-54.

32. *The Responsibilities of the Novelist* (New York, 1928), p. 164.

33. *Ibid.*

34. Frank Danby, "Mr. Harold Frederic's New Novel," *The Saturday Review* (March 21, 1896), 295-96. Frank Danby was the pen name of Julia Frankau, a friend of Frederic and his family.

Selected Bibliography

PRIMARY SOURCES

1. Bibliographies

BLANCK, JACOB (comp.). *Bibliography of American Literature*, III (New York, 1959), 217-23. Contains bibliographical descriptions of books that appeared over Frederic's name and pseudonyms.

WOODWARD, ROBERT H. "Harold Frederic: A Bibliography," *Studies in Bibliography*, Fredson Bowers, ed., XIII (Charlottesville, 1960), 247-57.

2. Texts

For publication information about Frederic's major works as well as some of his shorter works, consult the "Chronology," pp. 11-13, in this volume.

3. Manuscript Materials

The Harold Frederic Papers, Library of Congress. This collection contains miscellaneous manuscripts, notes, letters, and three appointment diaries. In addition it contains the Frederic will, several legal and financial records, and a few pictures.

The Papers of Grover Cleveland, Library of Congress. This collection contains numerous letters from Frederic to Cleveland and a few to Daniel S. Lamont, Cleveland's private secretary.

The Daniel S. Lamont Papers, Library of Congress. This collection contains a number of letters from Frederic to Lamont.

The Crane Collection, Butler Library, Columbia University. This collection includes two letters from Frederic to Stephen and Cora Crane. It contains about fifty letters written to Cora Crane, following Frederic's death, offering financial support for the Frederic children. The support was solicited by Cora Crane. Her respondents include G. B. Shaw, H. G. Wells, Henry James, Arthur Wing Pinero, Joseph Conrad, Conan Doyle, and other prominent men and women, both English and Irish.

4. Newspapers

A list of Frederic's newspaper stories would be far too long to include here. Significant and informative stories by and about Frederic can be found in the following newspapers during the years indicated:

Utica *Daily Observer,* 1878-1882
Utica *Morning Herald,* 1871, 1877, 1898
Albany *Evening Journal,* 1882-1884
New York *Times,* 1884-1898

SECONDARY SOURCES

Although no biography of Frederic has ever been published, the authors of the present volume are preparing a full-length biography for future publication. Of the items listed below, the dissertation by Paul Haines contains the greatest amount of reliable biographical information, as well as much perceptive criticism. Following is a partial list of books and articles in which Frederic and his work have been discussed. Many of them, as indicated, contain biographical inaccuracies that need correction.

ÅHNEBRINK, LARS. *The Beginnings of Naturalism in American Fiction.* Cambridge, Mass.: Harvard University Press, 1950. (Consult the Index for occasional pointed references to Frederic in this study, which is primarily concerned with the works of Hamlin Garland, Stephen Crane, and Frank Norris.)

ATHERTON, GERTRUDE. "Harold Frederic," *The Bookman* (London), XV (November, 1898), 15. (A brief but appreciative memoir.)

———. "The American Novel in England," *The Bookman,* XXX (February, 1910), 633-40. ("No American writer was ever more appreciated in England than Harold Frederic, and whatever he wrote was received by the press with the same consideration and distinction accorded to the leading British novelists. . . . The best men all read him, his books were seriously discussed, his next eagerly awaited.")

BEER, THOMAS. *Stephen Crane: A Study in American Letters.* With an Introduction by JOSEPH CONRAD. New York: A. A. Knopf, 1924. (Beer's verbal portrait of Frederic appears on pp. 150-52. See also Conrad's introduction for passing references to Frederic.)

BURLINGAME, ROGER. *Of Making Many Books: A Hundred Years of Reading, Writing and Publishing.* New York: Charles

Scribner's Sons, 1946. (This history of Scribner's, Frederic's first publisher, contains brief items of information about Frederic not available elsewhere. See especially pp. 5-6, 98-99, 132, and 211.)

CARTER, EVERETT. *Howells and the Age of Realism.* Philadelphia: Lippincott, 1954. (Contains a brief, but excellent chapter on Frederic, pp. 239-45. Inaccurate in its incidental biographical detail.)

———. "Introduction" to *The Damnation of Theron Ware.* Cambridge, Mass.: The Harvard University Press, 1960. (Carter's excellent critical introduction to this new edition is marred by factual, biographical errors. According to the introduction, for example, Frederic was born in 1859; the dust-jacket gives the date as 1858. Frederic was actually born on August 19, 1856.)

CRANE, STEPHEN. "Harold Frederic," *The Chap-Book,* VIII (March 15, 1898), 358-59.

———. *Letters,* edited by Robert W. Stallman and Lillian Gilkes. New York: New York University Press. (Consult the Index for many entries on Frederic and Kate Lyon.)

GILKES, LILLIAN. *Cora Crane: A Biography of Mrs. Stephen Crane.* Bloomington, Indiana: Indiana University Press, 1960. (Consult the Index for many entries on Frederic and Kate Lyon and for Cora Crane's part in Kate's life following Frederic's death.)

GREENE, NELSON. *History of the Mohawk Valley: Gateway to the West.* 4 vols. Chicago: S. J. Clarke Publishing Co., 1925. (See Vol. IV, 709-12, for a brief, interesting, but occasionally inaccurate biographical sketch of Frederic.)

GUINEY, LOUISE IMOGEN. "Harold Frederic: A Half-Length Sketch from the Life," *The Book Buyer,* XVII (January, 1899), 600-4.

HAINES, PAUL. "Harold Frederic." Unpublished dissertation (New York University, 1945).

HARRIS, FRANK. "Harold Frederic, *Ad Memoriam,*" *The Saturday Review* (London), LXXXVI (October 22, 1898), 526-28.

LOVETT, ROBERT MORSS. Introduction to *The Damnation of Theron Ware.* New York: Albert and Charles Boni, 1924.

MCWILLIAMS, CAREY. "Harold Frederic: A Country Boy of Genius," *University of California Chronicle,* XXV (1933), 21-34.

PARRINGTON, VERNON LOUIS. *Main Currents in American Thought.* New York: Harcourt, Brace, 1930. Vol. III, 288-89. (For comment on Parrington's criticism, see pp. 76-81 and 152-53 of the present volume.)

QUINN, ARTHUR HOBSON. *American Fiction.* New York: D. Appleton-Century, 1936. (See pp. 449-52 for what is perhaps the best comment on Frederic to be found in any of the standard literary histories.)

RALEIGH, JOHN HENRY. "The Damnation of Theron Ware," *American Literature,* XXX (May, 1958), 210-27. (A fine, thoughtful, and provocative analysis of Frederic's best-known novel.)

RAVITZ, ABE C. "Harold Frederic's Venerable Copperhead," *New York History,* XCI (January, 1960), 35-48. (A Study of Frederic's lifelong admiration for Horatio Seymour.)

"Some Recollections of Harold Frederic," *The Saturday Review* (London), LXXXVI (October 22, 1898), 571-72.

WALCUTT, CHARLES CHILD. "Harold Frederic and American Naturalism," *American Literature,* XI (March, 1939), 11-22.

———. *American Literary Naturalism: A Divided Stream.* Minneapolis: University of Minnesota Press, 1956. pp. 45-53. (In this, and in the preceding item, Professor Walcutt attempts, not altogether successfully, to place Frederic in the tradition of naturalism.)

WOODWARD, ROBERT H. "Harold Frederic: A Study of His Novels, Short Stories, and Plays." Indiana University, 1957. Unpublished dissertation.

———. "Harold Frederic and New York Folklore," *New York Folklore Quarterly,* XVI (Summer, 1960), 83-89.

Index

Names of characters and places in Frederic's works are followed by the title—in parentheses—of the work in which they appear.

Adams, John Quincy, 40
Adjutant Bacon Cadets, 32, 33, 35, 37
Advanced School (Utica, N.Y.), 27, 28, 29
Agnes, Mother (*The Return of the O'Mahony*), 100
Albany, N. Y., 18, 22, 45, 46, 47, 50, 51, 59, 82, 86
Albany *Evening Journal*, 46, 47, 48, 49, 50
Alexander III, Czar of Russia, 1881-94, 97
Ames, Oakes, 158
Ansdell, Richard (*Seth's Brother's Wife*), 48, 75, 76, 77, 79, 81
Apgar, Edgar Kelsey, 48, 49
Arnold, Matthew, 115, 116
Arthur, President Chester A., 47
Asbury, Francis, 115
Atherton, Gertrude, 147
Atlantic Monthly, The, 34, 35, 151
Bellamy, Edward, 128, 150, 158, 159; *Equality,* 150; *Looking Backward,* 150, 158
Bennett, Arnold, 139
Bierce, Ambrose, 105
Blandford, Marquess of, 122, 128
Bookman, The, 151
Boston *Herald,* The, 150
Bourget, Paul, 143
Boyce, Horace (*The Lawton Girl*), 91, 92, 93
Browne, Sir Thomas, 114, 117
Burgess, Gelett, 157
Burgin, G. B., 71
Burke's Peerage, 61
Burlingame, Edward L., 82, 83
Burlingame, Roger, 150
Burnett, Frances Hodgson, 158; *A Lady of Quality,* 158; *Little Lord Fauntleroy,* 158
Bush, Douglas, 114
Butler, Samuel, 146

Bailey, Elijah Prentiss, 36
Bailey, Frances (*Gloria Mundi* and *The Market-Place*), 120, 126, 127, 128, 129, 134
Balzac, Honoré de, 143
Barr, Robert, 60
Barrie, Sir James M., 61, 65, 161
Baxter, Francis Kernan, 32
Baxter, John, 21
Baxter, Joseph, 22
Beech, Abner (*The Copperhead*), 104, 105
Beekman, Abe (*Seth's Brother's Wife*), 48, 75, 77, 78, 79, 81
Campbell, Gerald, 65
Carlyle, Thomas, 95
Carter, Everett, 114, 153, 154
Century, The, 64
Chadwick, Edwin C., 120
Chance, Father (*The Lawton Girl*), 112
Chap-Book, The, 147
Chenango Canal, The, 37
Churchill, Sir Winston, 135
Clemens, Samuel L., 153
Cleveland, Grover, 47, 48, 49, 50, 51, 53, 54, 56, 64, 74, 78, 81, 88, 156

Conkling, Roscoe, 36, 37, 46, 47
Cook, Theodore Pease, 36, 45
Cooper, James Fenimore, 18, 29, 87
Cosmopolitan, The, 70, 109
Coventry, Sarah, 26
Crane, Cora, 68
Crane, Stephen, 20, 33, 68, 105, 106, 147, 152, 157, 158, 160, 161, 163; *Great Battles of the World,* 68; *Maggie,* 158, 160; *The Open Boat,* 160; *The Red Badge of Courage,* 158, 162
Crawford, F. Marion, 81
Cressage, Lady Edith (*Gloria Mundi* and *The Market-Place*), 124, 125, 132, 133, 134, 136, 137
Critic, The, 108, 148
Cross, Philip (*In the Valley*), 83, 84, 85, 86, 87, 88

Daily Chronicle, The, 148
Damuth, Captain Mark, 19
Darwin, Charles, 114, 115, 117
Daudet, Alphonse, 160
Davis, Richard Harding, 147, 158; *Soldiers of Fortune,* 158
Davitt, Michael, 46
Dayton, Charles Willoughby, 70
Deland, Margaret, 158; *John Ward, Preacher,* 158; *Philip and his Wife,* 158
DeMott, Helen, 27
DeMott, William, 23, 24, 27
Dickens, Charles, 29, 143
Dostoevski, Feodor Mikhailovich, 143
Dow, Lorenzo, 111
Doyle, Sir Arthur Conan, 61
Dreiser, Theodore, 158; *The Financier,* 158
Drumpipes, Earl of (*March Hares*), 119

Edinburgh Review, 147
Eggleston, Edward, 29, 158; *The Graysons,* 158
Emerson, Ralph Waldo, 20, 34
Erckmann, Emile—Chatrian, Alexandre, 28, 34, 38, 45, 73, 104, 142; *The Conscript,* 28; *Mme. Thérèse,* 28; *Waterloo,* 28
Erie Canal, The, 17, 22, 37, 117

Fairchild, Albert (*Seth's Brother's Wife*), 74, 75, 76, 79, 81, 92
Fairchild, Isabel (*Seth's Brother's Wife*), 75, 76, 79, 80
Fairchild, John (*Seth's Brother's Wife*), 74, 81
Fairchild, Seth (*Seth's Brother's Wife*), 74, 75, 76, 77, 78, 79, 80
Fisk, Jim, 158
Flaubert, Gustave, 160
Fleming, George, 65
Fletcher, A. E., 145
Folger, Charles J., 47
Forbes, Father (*The Damnation of Theron Ware*), 43, 113, 114, 115, 117, 156
Forman, Barry, 68, 98
Forman, Helen, 68
Forman, Heloise, 68
Forth, George (pseudonym of Harold Frederic), 118, 148
Fortnightly Review, 101, 102
Foxe, John, 143
Frederic, Grace Williams, 41, 46, 51, 62, 65, 66, 67, 68
Frederic, Harold, *see* Chronology *and* Contents

WRITINGS OF:
"The Blakelys of Poplar Place," 20, 38, 87
"Brother Sebastian's Friendship," 45
The Copperhead, 64, 104, 105, 142, 147, 152
"Cordelia and the Moon," 25, 112
The Damnation of Theron Ware (English title, *Illumination*), 17, 19, 25, 27, 33, 42, 62, 67, 70, 90, 107, 108, 109, 118,

130, 131, 132, 133, 142, 147, 148, 149, 150, 151, 152, 153, 157, 158, 161, 162, 163; critical study, 108-17
"A Day in the Wilderness," 106
"The Deserter," 27, 64, 105
"Down Among the Dead Men," 52
"Eve of the Fourth," 22, 26, 64, 106
Gloria Mundi (English reprint title, *Pomps and Vanities*), 62, 67, 70, 120, 130, 132, 133, 144, 149, 151, 152, 161; critical study, 120-30
"How Dickon Came by his Name," 144
In the Sixties, 57, 106, 142
In the Valley, 20, 28, 38, 41, 58, 95, 96, 110, 130, 144, 150, 151; critical study, 82-89
"The Jew's Christmas," 37, 38
The Lawton Girl, 58, 89, 110, 112, 142, 146, 150, 151, 153, 161; critical study, 89-96
March Hares, 62, 67, 120, 144, 148, 161; critical study, 118-20
The Market-Place, 66, 67, 120, 130, 144, 149, 162; critical study, 130-40
Marsena, 22, 32, 106, 142
"The Mohawk Valley during the Revolution," 39
Mrs. Albert Grundy, 64, 96, 120, 123, 156
The New Exodus, 70, 97
"Observations in Philistia," 64
"The Path of Murtogh," 144
The Return of the O'Mahony, 62, 63, 68, 103, 104, 144, 152, 156, 161, 162; critical study, 96-103
Seth's Brother's Wife, 17, 20, 36, 37, 42, 57, 58, 65, 82, 89, 90, 91, 92, 95, 96, 110, 142, 149, 152, 153, 161, 162; critical study, 73-82
"The Snarl," 63
"The Story of Peter Zarl," 38
"The War Widow," 64, 106
"Where Avon into Severn Flows," 144
The Young Emperor, 63, 96-97
Frederic, Harold Jr., 66
Frederic, Hereward, 66
Frederic, Ruby, 49, 64
Frederic, Ruth (Mrs. Eliot Keen), 45, 49, 65, 66, 72, 118
Frederick, Frances Ramsdell (also DeMott), 21, 22, 23, 24, 25, 33
Frederick, Henry, 19
Frederick, Henry DeMott, 19, 20, 21, 23
Frederick, Matilda, 19
Freeman, Mary Wilkins, 147
Fuller, Henry Blake, 162

Gardner, Abner B., 31
Garfield, President James A., 47
Garland, Hamlin, 77, 150, 157, 158, 160, 161, 162; *Main-Traveled Roads,* 158; *Rose of Dutcher's Coolly,* 158
Gissing, George, 139, 146, 159, 160; *The Emancipated,* 159; *New Grub Street,* 159
Gladstone, Sir William E., 64, 69, 103, 148
Glastonbury, Duke of (*Gloria Mundi*), 121
Godkin, E. L., 96
Gorki, Maxim, 143
Gould, Jay, 158
Grant, Ann, 28; *Memoirs of an American Lady,* 28
Grant, General Ulysses S., 26
Green, Beriah, 23, 41
Grove, DeWitt C., 36, 47
Gwynn, S. L., 147

Hagadorn, Jee (*The Copperhead*), 105
Haggard, Rider, 146, 159; *Allan Quartermain,* 159; *She,* 159

Haines, Paul, 80, 101, 153, 154
Hancock, Winfield Scott, 45
Hardy, Thomas, 141, 142, 143, 146, 160, 161; *Far From the Madding Crowd,* 143; *Jude the Obscure,* 142, 159; *The Mayor of Casterbridge,* 143; *A Pair of Blue Eyes,* 141, 143; *Return of the Native,* 141; *Tess of the d'Urbervilles,* 141, 142, 159; *Trumpet Major,* 143; *Under the Greenword Tree,* 141
Harper's New Monthly, 38, 39, 88
Harris, Frank, 60, 133, 148, 149
Hawthorne, Nathaniel, 20, 29, 57; *The Scarlet Letter,* 147
Healy, Tim, 102
Heinemann, William, 70, 71, 131, 152
Hemingway, Ernest, 157
Henley, W. E., 61, 161
Herkimer, Nicholas, 19, 83, 85, 86, 87
Higgins, Jerry (*The Return of the O'Mahony*), 98, 99, 100, 101
Holmes, Oliver Wendell, 34
Hope, Anthony, 159; *The Prisoner of Zenda,* 159; *Rupert of Hentzau,* 159
Hopkins, A. C., 31
Howe, John, 57, 59, 74, 82, 97, 102
Howells, William Dean, 29, 34, 35, 57, 88, 90, 128, 143, 144, 145, 147, 149, 150, 151, 154, 156, 158, 159, 160, 161; *Criticism and Fiction,* 150; *A Hazard of New Fortunes,* 154, 158; *A Modern Instance,* 162; *Rise of Silas Lapham,* 90, 162; *A Traveler from Altruria,* 159
Hughes, Spencer Leigh, 145

Illustrated London News, 64
Irving, Sir Henry, 55
Irving, Washington, 29

James, Henry, 145, 154, 155, 157
Johnson, Sir John (*In the Valley*), 85
Johnson, Dr. Samuel, 60, 61
Johnson, Sir William (*In the Valley*), 18, 83, 84, 85
Jones, Aunt Em ("The War Widow"), 106
Jones, Pomroy, 28; *Annals and Recollections of Oneida County,* 28
Josephus, 24

Kazin, Alfred, 80
Kennedy, Bart, 145
Kernan, Francis, 37
Kipling, Rudyard, 65
Kirkland, Joseph, 158, 162; *The McVeys,* 158; *Zury: The Meanest Man in Spring County,* 158

Lamont, Daniel S., 51, 56, 57, 74, 77, 156
Lane, John, 64
Lawton, Ben (*The Lawton Girl*), 91
Lawton, Jessica (*The Lawton Girl*), 90, 91, 94, 95
Ledsmar, Dr. (*The Damnation of Theron Ware*), 20, 113, 115, 116
Lincoln, Abraham, 22
Linkhaw, Archie; *see* Drumpipes, Earl of
Linsky (Lynch) (*The Return of the O'Mahony*), 102
London, Jack, 158
Lossing, Benson G., 28; *Life and Times of Philip Schuyler,* 28; *Pictorial Field Books,* 28; *Pictorial History of the Civil War,* 28
Lowell, James Russell, 34
Lyon, Kate, 67, 68, 72, 118

McQuade, Catherine, 43
McQuade, James, 26

McQuade, Josephine, 43
McQuade, Thomas, 43
Madden, Celia (*The Damnation of Theron Ware* and *The Market-Place*), 43, 113, 115, 116, 132, 133, 134, 136, 148, 156
Mallarmé, Stéphane, 65
Man, 93 (New York periodical)
Manchester Guardian, The, 148
Marlborough, Duke of, 122
Marsena (*Marsena*), 106
Maupassant, Guy de, 143
Mauverensen, Douw (*In the Valley*), 20, 83, 84, 85, 86, 87, 91
Meredith, George, 143, 146, 159; *The Amazing Marriage,* 159; *Rhoda Fleming,* 148
Mérimée, Prosper, 28; *History of Peter the Cruel,* 28
Meynell, Alice, 65
Miller, Charles, R., 51, 65
Minster, Kate (*The Lawton Girl*), 91, 92, 94
Minster, Stephen (*The Lawton Girl*), 91, 92, 94
Mitchell, Edward P., 50
Moltke, Field Marshal von, 29
Montaigne, Michel Eyquem de, 67, 114; *Essays,* 67
Moore, George, 159, 160, 161; *Esther Waters,* 159; *Evelyn Innes,* 159
More, Sir Thomas, 126
Morris, William, 128, 135, 159; *The House of the Wolfings,* 159; *News From Nowhere,* 159; *The Story of the Glittering Plain,* 159; *The Well at the World's End,* 159
Mosscrop, David (*March Hares*), 119, 123
Mundy, L. C., 31, 35
Murphy (*The Return of the O'Mahony*), 102

Nation, The, 120, 150, 151
National Observer, The, 64, 65, 96
Nevins, Allan, 48
New York *Times,* 49, 50, 52, 54, 55, 56, 58, 59, 61, 63, 64, 65, 67, 68, 97, 146, 156, 163
Newland, John, 19
Nietzsche, Friedrich, 135, 136, 137, 138; *Beyond Good and Evil,* 135; *Thus Spake Zarathustra,* 135
Norris, Frank, 158, 160, 161, 162; *McTeague,* 161; *A Man's Woman,* 161; *The Pit,* 158; *The Responsibilities of a Novelist,* 161

O'Connor, T. P., 57
O'Connor, Mrs. T. P., 149
O'Daly, Cormac (*The Return of the O'Mahony*), 98, 99, 100, 101, 102
O'Donnell, Captain Joseph, 32
O'Mahony, Bernard (*The Return of the O'Mahony*), 101, 102
O'Mahony, Mrs. Fergus (*The Return of the O'Mahony*), 100
O'Mahony, Kate (*The Return of the O'Mahony,* 100, 101, 102
Oneida Historical Society, 39
Oriskany, Battle of, 19, 39, 40, 84, 86, 87
Oswego, N. Y., 23, 67

Pall Mall Budget, 66
Pall Mall Gazette, 53, 66
Parnell, Charles Stewart, 46
Parrington, Vernon Louis, 76, 77, 152, 153; *Main Currents of American Thought,* 152, 153
Parshall, Job ("The Deserter"), 27
Partridge, Bernard, 61, 161
Pater, Walter, 111, 115, 117
Paulding, James Kirke, 87
Pawling, Sydney S., 70
Peaussier, Vestalia; *see* Skinner, Vestalia
Peck, Harry Thurston, 108, 109, 151
Peck, Bishop Jesse Truesdell, 33
Pennell, Joseph, 61, 65

Pflanz, Arthur, 29, 34, 37
Pierce, Loren (*The Damnation of Theron Ware*), 113
Pinero, Sir Arthur Wing, 55
Plowden, Lord (*The Market-Place*), 135, 136, 137
Porlock (*Gloria Mundi*), 124
Punch, 61

Raleigh, John Henry, 154
Ramsdale, Moses, 19
Ramsdell, Lucretia Newland, 19, 21, 22, 24, 33
Richie, Frank, 67
Richie, Mary (May) Lyon, 67
Robins, Elizabeth, 65
Robinson, Edwin Arlington, 108, 109
Ruskin, John, 111, 115, 128

St. John's Church (Utica), 42, 43, 44, 46
Saturday Evening Post, The, 130, 162
Saturday Review, The (London), 71, 148
Scott, Sir Walter, 29
Scribner, Charles, 149, 150
Scribner's Magazine, 57, 64, 74, 82, 83, 90
Semple, Colin (*The Market-Place*), 131
Seymour, Horatio, 23, 25, 26, 27, 40, 41, 43, 48, 73, 78, 82, 84
Shaw, George Bernard, 146, 160
Shorter, Clement, 60, 61, 64
Sketch, The, 60
Skinner, Adele (*March Hares*), 119
Skinner, Mr. (*March Hares*), 119
Skinner, Vestalia (Peaussier) (*March Hares*), 119, 120
Soulsby, Sister (*The Damnation of Theron Ware*), 117, 156
Spectator, The, 147
Spencer, Herbert, 96, 114
Squires, Milton (*Seth's Brother's Wife*), 42, 75
Steven, Robert, 149
Stevenson, Robert Louis, 65, 159; *The Black Arrow,* 159; *The Master of Ballantrae,* 159
Stewart, Daisy (Desideria) (*In the Valley*), 83, 84, 88
Stewart, Mr. (*In the Valley*), 83, 88
Stokes, Frederick A., 131
Stokes, John Scott, 71
Stone and Kimball, 70, 109
Stone, Herbert S., 70
Stone, Williams L., 39; *The Life of Joseph Brant,* 39
Stratford, Miss ("The Eve of the Fourth"), 26, 106
Street, G. S., 65
Sumner, William Graham, 93, 94, 96; *What Social Classes Owe to Each Other,* 93

Taylor, Walter F., 95
Tenney, Schuyler (*The Lawton Girl*), 92, 93, 94
Terry, Father Edward A., 42, 43, 44, 45, 46, 97, 110
Terry, Ellen, 55
Teymouth, John Jost, 18
Thackeray, William M., 29, 161; *Henry Esmond,* 58, 82, 88
Thorpe, Alfred (*The Market-Place*), 139
Thorpe, Joel Stormont (*The Market-Place*), 66, 131, 132, 133, 134, 135, 136, 137, 138, 139, 158
Thorpe, Julia (*The Market-Place*), 139
Thorpe, Louisa (*The Market-Place*), 135, 139
Tilden, Samuel J., 36, 48, 78
Tisdale, Zeke (The O'Mahony) (*The Return of the O'Mahony*), 97, 98, 99, 100, 101, 102, 103
Tocqueville, Alexis, Comte de, 92
Tolstoy, Leo Nikolaevich, 143, 160

Torr, Augustine (*Gloria Mundi*), 124, 125, 129, 135
Torr, Duke of (*Gloria Mundi*), 121, 123, 124, 125
Torr, Edward (*Gloria Mundi*), 124, 125, 129, 135
Torr, Emanuel (*Gloria Mundi*), 120, 125, 126, 127, 134
Torr, Lord Julius (*Gloria Mundi*), 120, 123, 124, 125
Tower, Christian (*Gloria Mundi* and *The Market-Place*), 120, 123, 124, 125, 126, 127, 128, 129, 133, 134, 135, 140
Tracy, Reuben (*The Lawton Girl*), 91, 92, 93, 94
Twain, Mark; *see* Clemens, Samuel L.

Utica, N. Y., 17-49, 59, 65, 97, 104, 110, 111
Utica *Morning Herald,* 35, 36, 39, 47
Utica *Observer,* 29, 36, 37, 38, 39, 42, 43, 44, 45, 46, 47, 49, 50, 57, 81, 144

Victoria, Queen of England, 135

Walpole, Horace, 28; *Memoirs of the Reign of King George III,* 28
Ward, Mrs. Humphrey, 146, 158, 159; *Marcella,* 159; *Robert Elsmere,* 158, 159
Ward, Lester, 93, 94, 96; *Dynamic Sociology,* 93
Ware, Alice (*The Damnation of Theron Ware*), 42
Ware, Theron (*The Damnation of Theron Ware*), 44, 111, 112, 113, 114, 115, 116, 117, 133, 148
Warner, Charles Dudley, 142
Warren, Arthur, 54, 60
Watson, Aaron, 54, 55, 57, 61, 145, 149; *A Newspaper Man's Memories,* 54
Watson, Sir Alfred, 145
Waugh, Arthur, 108
Weed, Thurlow, 47
Weekly Echo, 57
Wells, Henry George, 65, 146
Wendover (*The Lawton Girl*), 92, 93, 94
Wesley, John, 25, 111, 115
Westminster Gazette, The, 148
When Knighthood Was in Flower, 150
Whipple, Mose ("The Deserter"), 105
Willey, Basil, 114
Williams, Grace, *see* Frederic, Grace Williams
Williams, Ruth, 41
Woodward, Robert H., 101, 154
Workman, Mr. (*Seth's Brother's Wife*), 81

Yeats, William Butler, 65
Yerkes, Charles T., 158

Zangwill, Israel, 109
Zola, Émile, 160, 161